Thieves, Liars and Mountaineers

On the 8,000m peak circus in Pakistan

MARK HORRELL

Published by Mountain Footsteps Press

First published as an ebook 2012
Revised edition published 2017

ISBN (paperback): 978-0-9934130-8-7
ISBN (ebook): 978-0-9934130-7-0

"I knew that Dr. Cook had not climbed Mount McKinley. Barrill had told me so and in addition I knew it in the same way that any New Yorker would know that no man could walk from the Brooklyn Bridge to Grant's tomb in ten minutes."

Belmore Browne

THIEVES, LIARS AND MOUNTAINEERS

Footsteps on the Mountain
Travel Diaries

DAY 1
A TOURIST IN PAKISTAN

Thursday, 11 June 2009 – Skardu, Karakoram, Pakistan

Well, we made it to Skardu in one piece, even if we didn't arrive in the manner we'd intended. After two cancelled flights from Islamabad we made the collective decision to drive up the Karakoram Highway instead. We arrived stiff-limbed and sore-necked at 1.30am last night after two full days on the road. We have a rest day here to stretch our joints before continuing in jeeps tomorrow.

Despite the heightened security situation since my previous visit to Pakistan two years ago, I've found it more relaxing this time around, probably because I'm getting used to the country now. Perceptions of Pakistan in the West are that they dislike westerners here, but I've found the people nothing but friendly, if a little curious about foreigners.

Foreign tourists are something of a rarity here. Kate and Anna, two of our K2 trekking party, were asked by a woman in a restaurant in Islamabad to have her photograph taken with them. Then, at the Daman-e-Koh viewpoint above the city the following day, we all received the same treatment. A man asked to have his photo taken with the whole team. Kate then suffered the discomfort of being stared at by a passenger on a bus while we waited in a traffic jam in Rawalpindi. She found it disturbing and unreasonable, but women dress differently in Pakistan. I wonder if the passenger was accustomed to seeing a bare-headed woman in short sleeves, or whether it was a bit like a topless woman sitting in a traffic jam in New York.

Strangest of all was when we stopped for fruit at a roadside market a few hours up the Karakoram Highway. We'd been advised to keep a low profile, but Arian and Gorgan's bright orange trekking tops and lime-green shorts didn't fit this description. I'm guessing such flamboyant dress is rarely seen at markets in North-West Frontier Province. Our driver decided it was a suitable moment to carry out some routine repairs to the vehicle. Half an hour later we were feeling liked caged zoo animals as a hundred-strong crowd of beggars, hawkers, curious onlookers and at least one police officer gathered round to peer at the exotic wildlife inside our bus. Everything felt pretty relaxed, though, and at no point did I feel in any danger.

Islamabad felt more liberal than the other parts of Pakistan we passed through. A brand-new city was planned and built on a grid system in the 1960s. It's a bit like Milton Keynes, but warmer. Tree-lined dual carriageways bounding rectangular blocks of rectangular buildings, are divided into commercial and residential sectors.

During our drive up the Karakoram Highway we saw women very rarely, and they always wore long sleeves and had their heads covered. Full burkhas covering all but the eyes seem to be extremely rare. On the Karakoram Highway, the *shalwar kameez* is the standard clothing for both men and women. This comprises a loose-fitting top and loose-fitting trousers. In Islamabad western dress is common, though perhaps less so for women. In Islamabad women do walk around openly though.

We stayed at a standard tourist hotel in one of the commercial sectors. Despite the armed guard outside, I felt confident enough wandering among the various shops and restaurants in our block. Women in Islamabad appear to be comfortable talking to men without shame or embarrassment, but I don't remember ever speaking to a Pakistani woman outside of Pakistan's capital city. In one restaurant in Islamabad a waitress even felt confident enough to joke with Phil Crampton, our expedition leader, when he asked for a medium steak.

'Do you want it half done?' she asked.

'No, I want you to cook the whole thing,' he replied. He didn't realise that by 'half done' she meant 'medium'.

She started laughing at him. 'But of course we will cook the whole thing, sir, but how long would you like us to cook it for?'

The drive up the Karakoram Highway is long but picturesque, becoming gradually more dramatic as we progress northwards. Beginning on green fertile plains and wide carriageways around Islamabad, the road heads north into the mountains, passing through towns and villages as it climbs through alpine pine forests. Eventually it reaches the banks of the wide Indus River and contours high along its gorge. For the first eight hours of the drive the road is heavily populated, which creates a problem for Kate and Anna, who are unable to get out for a pee for fear of attracting an audience.

We stop for the night in the town of Besham in the district of Swat. This is one of the areas of Pakistan currently considered a security risk – government forces are fighting a war against the Taliban nearby – but we arrive after nightfall, stay in a secure hotel behind a guarded compound, and are away by six o'clock the following morning.

Beyond Besham the terrain becomes steadily more arid, the mountains more jagged and dramatic. Sadly, by the time we pass Nanga Parbat, the ninth highest mountain in the world, towering 7km above us, the sky has clouded over and a dust storm is brewing. I had good views of the mountain last time I came this way, but this time we continue past, grabbing only occasional glimpses. At seven o'clock in the evening we turn off the main highway and continue to follow the Indus to Skardu. The gorge has narrowed considerably and the rocky hillsides hug us on both sides. Night falls quickly, hiding this impressive terrain for the remainder of the journey.

After lunch today we repack our kit and organise porter loads for the trek. I rearrange my two kit bags. I fill one with climbing gear that can go straight to Base Camp. The maximum porter load is 25kg, but porters are paid the same wage regardless of the size of their load, so we spend some time optimising our loads so that none of this quota is wasted. Over a hundred porters will transport our equipment to Base Camp, so it would get considerably more expensive if we didn't do this. I have a 3kg Poisk oxygen cylinder thrown into my bag to bring its weight up to 25kg.

Afterwards I wander around Skardu with Ian, a friend from a previous expedition to the North Col of Everest, and Gordon, a diminutive self-deprecating Canadian with a fine line in sarcasm. Skardu, like Leh in Northern India, is a trekking and climbing centre lying in a picturesque setting on the banks of the Indus River. It's an oasis of poplars and eucalyptus trees in the desert, surrounded by high, rocky mountains. Unlike Leh, however, the shops are a bit more traditional, selling all sorts of junk but little in the way of trekking and climbing gear. There are no restaurants; and, of course, no bars in a country where alcohol is illegal.

There are a number things to do in the surrounding area, like visiting nearby lakes or a fort up on a cliff above the town. There's plenty of potential for Skardu to be a buzzing tourist centre serving the Karakoram, but this potential has not yet been realised – and it doesn't look like happening any time soon. Today, it's hot, dry and dusty. Cars hare up and down the single main street, and it isn't a particularly pleasant stroll. I decide to go back to my room at the Masherbrum Hotel and read my book.

In the evening the clouds draw in, the wind picks up and it's noticeably colder. Something I've eaten has disagreed with me, and just before dinner I start vomiting. The food I force down at dinner comes straight back up again. On the bright side, if I'm going to have funny things happening to my stomach it's best to get them out of the way right at the beginning of the trip.

DAY 2
A HAIR-RAISING JEEP RIDE

Friday, 12 June 2009 – Askole, Karakoram, Pakistan

It's our last day in vehicles today, and for the rough dirt track to Askole we switch to Toyota Land Cruisers. Ian and I share an open-sided soft top with Bob, a tall, retired gentleman from California. He is softly spoken, and has come to do the K2 base camp trek alongside our expedition team.

The drive doesn't get off to a good start. Our driver stops the vehicle and opens the bonnet of the jeep at the very first checkpoint, not half an hour out of Skardu, and discovers that we're leaking brake fluid. Gorgan wanders over from another vehicle for a look.

'It's leaking all over the road,' he says, peering cheerfully into our back passenger seat. 'But don't worry. It's better not to think about it.'

'You should take out your ice axes,' says Arian, with a big grin on his face, 'so that you can arrest the vehicle in the event of a fall.'

'We have no brakes?' I ask the driver when he gets back in the vehicle to drive away.

'It's OK,' he says. 'I once drove all the way from Askole to Skardu with no brakes, and no problem.'

This isn't the most reassuring thing he could have said, and it makes Arian's suggestion sound helpful.

We pass through irrigated villages lined with avenues of poplar trees and fields of rice. We are driving through an area populated by Ismaelis. These are followers of a more moderate branch of Islam than the rest of Pakistan. After seeing hardly any women at all for the last three days, the area is now full of women in colourful clothing, walking along the road and working the fields.

As we ascend to Askole the road becomes rougher, and narrows to a single track winding high above a river gorge. We have to stop and reverse several times when we meet vehicles coming the other way. We have a stand-off with an army vehicle at a particularly precarious section. The two drivers stop and eyeball each other, neither willing to reverse. A soldier carrying a big gun gets out of the back and walks over to remonstrate with our driver, who maintains his cool and refuses to budge. The soldier slowly struts behind us to examine the road. Then he walks back to his own vehicle and examines the road behind it, before getting back inside.

A moment later the army vehicle reverses and we nudge past. 'Our driver has balls of steel,' says Ian.

A few minutes later, with a sheer drop just inches to our left, our vehicle gets a soaking when a waterfall tumbles down from the cliff to our right. The shower sprinkles a liberal quantity of mud inside the vehicle. The front windscreen is now almost totally obscured by a muddy film, but our driver is undeterred. He keeps going with a precipice to our left. A couple of minutes later, when the track widens, he stops to clean the windscreen.

Gorgan was right – it's better not to think about it. But we arrive safely in Askole at 5.30, eight hours after leaving Skardu, and drive into a campsite behind a walled compound. The village sits on a sloping hillside a few hundred metres above the Braldu River. It is enclosed on both sides by high, rocky cliffs. The land is dry and dusty, but the village is well irrigated. There are plenty of trees and lush green fields between the dust slopes.

Phil described Askole as a 'shithole'. I was expecting a rural village, spoiled by western commercialisation in the way villages at trailheads often are: crowded tin and concrete shacks selling plastic junk, inhabited by aggressive salesmen. The children have been tainted by tourists dishing out rupees, sweets and pens, and beg unpleasantly, but the village itself is authentic and unspoiled. Flat-roofed mud houses with square compounds have been built one on top of another on the dusty slopes. Water flows through irrigation channels alongside narrow passageways between houses.

Salman, our trekking guide, takes us to a small heritage museum inside one of the houses. Wooden pillars hold up the mud roof, and a wooden ladder through a trapdoor leads down into an underground level. The family lives down here in winter, when temperatures can reach as low as -20°C. It feels more like a stable than a home, with a hay-lined area sectioned off by a low fence; but it feels cosy, and it is here the family sleeps. A mud-brick stove and pots in one corner of the chamber form the kitchen area.

This is our first evening camping, and we have good food in our dining tent tonight. Gordon likes it so much that at one point he puts too much food in his mouth and takes ten minutes to finish chewing it. Ian, Arian and Kate can't eat either because they are laughing uncontrollably until he swallows the last mouthful.

DAY 3
FIRST DAY OF THE TREK

Saturday, 13 June 2009 – Jhola, Concordia Trek, Pakistan

The first day of the expedition starts at six o'clock with 130 porters assembling in the compound and fighting over our loads. We stand and watch for some time, but at eight o'clock I get bored and start up the trail with some of the others in the group.

Today's walk is best described by three words: sun, dust and sand. For six hours we walk along the wide desert gorge of the Braldu, sometimes on a path carved in a cliff face above the river, sometimes across stony ground, but mostly across flat sandy plains. Most of the time I amble along at my own pace, but the presence of our 130 porters – and those of other expeditions bound for K2, Broad Peak and the Gasherbrums – means that the path is full of traffic. I glimpse occasional views of snow-capped peaks between clouds, but most of the big mountains are further along the trail.

I walk for a time with Gordon and Arian. Gordon bought a bright orange umbrella in Skardu to keep off the sun, and Arian and I laugh when he first brings it out. Arian is a French environmental student who tells me his main focus for the expedition is not the summit of Gasherbrum II like the rest of us, but to clear Camp 4 of detritus from previous expeditions. He carries a handheld video camera, and shoots monologues of himself as he walks along.

At one point I see him filming a stream with litter on its banks, and decide to make my own contribution.

'Fucking disgraceful, isn't it,' I shout, clapping him on the back as I walk behind him.

Rock hewn pathway approaching Jhola campsite

I look back, but his dark expression suggests this may not make it into the final cut.

Jhola campsite is at an altitude of 3,150m, and is built into sandy platforms above a major tributary of the Braldu River. I recognise it from afar by the grey plastic Portaloos that cover the area alongside camp. I arrive at 2.30pm but have to wait another two hours for all our tents and kit to arrive with the porters.

Salman our trekking guide is having trouble with his knee. Gordon, a paramedic, summons Gorgan, an osteopath, to take a look and give it his considered opinion. It doesn't take Gorgan long to realise the injury is not serious, and he says it can be treated with a poultice doused in alcohol tied around the knee joint. There's just one problem: we're in Pakistan, and alcohol is not so easy to come by. I've not had a whiff of it since arriving in Islamabad.

While Gorgan goes in search of the remedy I try to persuade Gordon that a few members of the team have much the same problem as Salman

'Hey, Gordon. If he manages to find any alcohol, he should obtain quite a lot of it as a precaution.'

He ignores me. I have a feeling he isn't treating my request with the seriousness it deserves.

DAY 4
DUSTY MONOTONY

Sunday, 14 June 2009 – Paiyu, Concordia Trek, Pakistan

An early but efficient start today. Ian nudges me awake at 5.30, and by six o'clock we have not only packed all our things, but have put away the tent as well. Still, I'm the last of our team to leave Jhola campsite at 6.45 after I've breakfasted and washed. Apart from Bob, Gombu, and our liaison officer Major Iqbal of the Pakistan Army, whom I overtake about an hour out of camp, it's the last I see of the rest of them until I reach Paiyu campsite in the afternoon.

About fifty metres out of camp I hear voices behind me, and it seems all 130 of our porters have decided to leave camp together. I step out of the way and let them all pass, but for the rest of the day I find myself leapfrogging them every few minutes. They walk more quickly than me, but only in short bursts before they have to stop and take a rest. I often find myself stepping off the path to let a group pass, only to see them stop again just a few metres later.

In this way my walk continues for the next seven hours. The scenery is dramatic enough, but monotonous. I continue to follow the Braldu River, a wide grey steep-sided valley that snakes its narrow path along a broad flood plain. The path alternates from dusty trail to sandbank to pebble-strewn beach. Occasionally the trail is cut high into the left-hand wall, but usually it keeps to the valley floor. I'm in and out of sun all day, as the clouds close in above the valley sides and keep the mountains hidden from view. The grand mountain views are still to come, and for the moment I have to be content with this dusty valley.

I reach Paiyu campsite at 1.30pm. It's in a sheltered spot among broad-leaved trees, but it's as dusty as everywhere else. It will be our home as we acclimatise for a day and a couple of nights. Although we've only been walking for two days and climbed just 350m, we're already at an altitude of 3,400m and need to let our bodies adjust.

At dinner this evening we discuss sleeping arrangements. Gordon now has a tent to himself and is feeling abandoned. Some people prefer their own tent, while others prefer to share.

'You can sleep with Ian if you like,' I suggest.

'Are you pimping me?' Ian replies.

'I'll offer you two sheep and a goat,' Gordon says.

'It's a deal,' I reply.

'But what's in it for you?' Arian asks, looking in my direction.

'Well, I now have a tent to myself and a goat.'

Before I realise what I've said, everyone is roaring with laughter.

DAY 5
CLIMBING BIG MOUNTAINS

Monday, 15 June 2009 – Paiyu, Concordia Trek, Pakistan

We have a rest day at Paiyu camp to help us acclimatise before climbing above 4,000m tomorrow. At morning tea, Anna's husband Philippe, who has set himself the formidable target of climbing Gasherbrum II (G2), Gasherbrum I (G1) and Broad Peak this season, produces his research into the three mountains. He's put together a little pack containing details of the trek into Gasherbrum Base Camp, day-by-day summit routes with camps, and photographs of the various climbs.

It's great reading, though I feel less confident about G1 after reading it. The introductory paragraph says that only 265 people have climbed it to date, and then it has this to say:

'It also has the lowest death rate of any of the 8,000m peaks, though this may be because only really experienced mountaineers would consider attempting a mountain as technical as Gasherbrum I.'

Hmm… make that really experienced mountaineers, and me.

The crux of the climb is the Japanese Couloir, a four-to-eight-hour ascent on fixed ropes of slopes at an angle of forty-five to fifty-five degrees. This is steep – and Phil, who has climbed it, adds that parts are up to seventy degrees. I know that I will struggle on this terrain, and may well find it beyond my abilities. The positive side is that we'll be tackling it after G2, and I'm sure a successful ascent of G2 followed by some rest will boost my confidence no end.

Philippe, who has climbed Everest, will be attempting the three summits 'unsupported'. I'm not exactly sure what this means. He's only paying for base camp services from Phil, but he has hired Serap Jangbu Sherpa to climb with him. He will be doing more load carrying than the rest of us, and digging his own tent pitches, something we're intending to leave to our 'dream team' – Phil's description of our team of Sherpas: Tarke, Pasang Gombu, Pasang Lama and Temba. I know from experience that digging out a flat area of snow to pitch your tent is an exhausting task at extreme altitudes.

Whether Philippe will also be helping to fix the ropes on some of the more technical sections, I don't know. When many teams are together on a mountain, they usually share resources and cooperate with the rope fixing. So-called 'independent' climbers rarely take part in the rope fixing, although they often make use of the ropes. They are sometimes asked to make a contribution, either financial or by providing ropes and anchors. But there is not much the rope-fixing teams can do if they refuse. In Philippe's case, he is paying Serap Jangbu's salary, and Serap will be helping to fix ropes.

Our conversation turns to how much support you should take on an expedition. Phil believes in making life at Base Camp comfortable, so that his climbers conserve their energy and are in the best possible shape for the climb.

He tells us about an incident on Everest this year when a climber purchased 'base camp only' services from Phil's company Altitude Junkies, and hired no additional Sherpa support. His plan was to do all his own load carrying, dig the platforms, pitch his tent, and do all his own cooking. He wanted to be able to say he'd climbed Everest unsupported.

He reached the summit under his own steam, but he was so exhausted that he got into difficulties on the way down. He was helped back down the mountain by other teams, was badly frostbitten, and will probably need to have fingers and toes amputated.

Some people would argue that if you need help getting down, then you have not climbed a mountain unsupported. After all, to complete an ascent, you have to do the whole route in both directions. It's virtually impossible to carry an unconscious person at those altitudes. He must have been able to assist his evacuation by walking (or staggering), but it seems probable he would be dead without the help of others.

There are those who consider it an honourable thing to climb unsupported. But is it fair on the climbing teams and the Sherpas who work tirelessly to help when things go wrong? On a mountain as busy as Everest there will always be people who will help a climber in danger if they can, but their assistance shouldn't be taken for granted.

I have a different climbing philosophy. I prefer comfort on expeditions – you're supposed to be on holiday, after all. The eight porters, four kitchen staff and two guides that my climbing partner Mark Dickson and I hired for our Mera and Island Peak expedition last month might seem extravagant, but we completed the climbs with minimum fuss, and camping was no hardship for us. We could simply appreciate the scenery and enjoy ourselves.

Gordon tells me about an expedition he once organised to Baruntse, near Makalu in Nepal. It's a mountain that Mark and I walked past during our expedition. To save on costs, Gordon told the Nepalese trekking agency handling his logistics that they would do without a kitchen tent and kitchen crew.

'And then the fuckers brought a cook and kitchen tent for the porters,' Gordon says. 'Every night they dined in comfort while we were trying to get MSR stoves working in the porch of our tent. Man, I'm never doing that again. And we didn't get much above Camp 1, so the whole expedition was a bit of a farce.'

I spend most of today reading my book. There seems to be a bit of competition going on for the attentions of Kate. Yesterday, while I was ambling slowly with Bob and Major Iqbal, everyone else shot off ahead and reached camp long before us. I ask Gordon, who's a few years older, why he was walking so quickly. There is no point in overexerting at this stage of the expedition, as it usually leads to altitude sickness. We have two months ahead of us, and there is no rush.

'Well, I know it's better to go a little slower,' he replies candidly, 'but I didn't want Kate to think I couldn't keep up.'

In the mess tent, Gordon, Arian, Ian and Kate play cards for forfeits instead of cash. The forfeits include making bed tea and carrying water for each other on the trek. I sit alongside them reading my book and I get accused of being a spoilsport.

'Why would I want to get up at 5.30 to make tea for one of you jokers?' I say.

When I finally join in, I have a lucky streak and beat them easily. I end the afternoon with the wholly erroneous reputation of being a card genius, which I'm only going to maintain by not playing again.

DAY 6
ONTO THE BALTORO GLACIER

Tuesday, 16 June 2009 – Urdukas, Concordia Trek, Pakistan

Today promises much, but delivers little as we continue up the valley in the direction of Concordia. This is supposed to be one of the world's great treks, with giant rock towers and ice peaks rising all around us, but we've seen little of them so far. Leaving Paiyu camp shortly after 6.30 this morning, I expect to be in shade for the first hour. But when the sun rises above the mountains, I'm certain I will be slapping on the sun cream, donning my sun hat and walking in sweltering heat for the rest of the day. This is not what happens.

There is one positive: when we reach the Baltoro Glacier, just a few minutes out of camp, we climb away from the dust that has plagued us for the last three days. From its beginning on the left-hand side of the valley, the path slants up and across to the right as it climbs up the snout of the glacier and onto moraine. I amble along at my own pace again, slower than everybody except Bob and the major. With no view beyond the clouds that close around me, the day passes in tedium as I climb up and down moraine-strewn ice ridges. I stop constantly to let porters pass. I put on my jacket when a snow shower begins, only to take it off again when the sun peeps through cloud.

There is one brief moment of excitement. I'm on a narrow path climbing a scree slope, and some fool of a muleteer sends his horses down in the opposite direction before I've reached the top. There is nowhere for me to get out of the way, and the first horse panics as it approaches. There is a steep drop below, on a path far too narrow for it to turn around. I hurl expletives up the slope, screaming at its master not to let any more horses down. I breath in and squeeze as tightly against the slope as I can. There isn't room on the path for both me and the horse, and it has to run straight over me to get past. It's a big horse – if it steps on my feet that's probably my expedition over.

I hold my breath. The first horse rushes past, bumping against me, but missing my feet. The second horse does likewise. I look up expecting to see more, but the others have been held back at the top of the traverse. I breathe a sigh of relief and hurry to the top. I'm furious with the muleteer, but I pass by without looking at him. I had a fright, and I'm in a bad mood for the next few hundred metres.

I reach Urdukas campsite at 2.30pm. Perched on a grassy bank above the glacier, it rises in terraces sectioned off by scrubby bushes. It's our last haven of greenery for two months.

My arrival is timely: all our tents have already been erected by my fellow team members, and tea and biscuits are waiting for me. I spend a pleasant hour rehydrating and looking out across the glacier from our lofty perch.

Evening meals in the mess tent have become an arena for Gordon's wise-cracking. He's an entertaining character, but everything he says goes in one ear and out the other. This is quite a garrulous group. Ian, Philippe and I are much the quietest members, sitting quietly while everyone else talks nonsense around us.

DAY 7
ICE AND PORTERS

Wednesday, 17 June 2009 – Gore II, Concordia Trek, Pakistan

This morning begins with a porter strike. It's snowing when we get up at our usual time of 5.30 and pack the tents away. Everything is wet and covered with mud. As we finish our breakfast in the mess tent, we learn that the porters don't intend to leave camp until the snow has stopped.

'This is ridiculous,' Anna says. She has only come here on a two-week trek and doesn't have as much time as the rest of us. 'Supposing it snows for four days, what then?'

Gorgan is more outspoken. 'The porters are cry babies,' he says. 'They should go home to their mothers.'

Phil thinks it's a ploy to get a bigger tip, but it's more likely to have the opposite effect.

We huddle in a cold mess tent for an hour and a half. When the snow finally stops and we leave camp at 8.15, I've lost sympathy for the porters. On previous days their start has been staggered, but now all 500 of them, from several expedition teams, leave camp at the same time.

Now if I move off the trail to let anyone by, as I've been doing on previous days, I find a hundred porters lining up behind. Of course, no one will let me back in line again, and I have to wait several minutes before I can resume my walk.

I stop letting them past, and this starts to annoy them as a line builds up behind me.

'Excuse me, sir', I keep hearing over my shoulder.

I keep going, because I know that I will have to wait a long time if I stop. I become resentful that they are only carrying 25kg each, which in Nepal would be considered little more than a basket of heavy shopping. Although it would exhaust me, it is not much for a porter who has been carrying loads for all his life. They walk in bursts, stopping more frequently than the number 19 bus during rush hour, and I have to keep letting the same porters past again and again. The concept of walking more slowly and stopping less frequently doesn't seem to have been invented yet. As for overtaking – well, it seems to be much less trouble for them to wait for me to step off the path. I should be enjoying the scenery, but instead I just find myself thinking about porters.

In the meantime the snow returns and the views are nonexistent. It's a monotonous glacier trudge once again, up and down over rocks. The terrain is not quite as difficult as yesterday, but there's a lot of boulder-hopping. Porters and crappy weather dominate my day, and the hours pass in grinding tedium.

Army of porters and trekkers on the Baltoro Glacier

I reach Gore II camp, in the middle of the glacier, at 1.30. The sun threatens to come out, and for the first time in five days we have tantalising glimpses of the mountains around us. We've now walked past the Trango Towers and Masherbrum without catching so much as a sneaky peek at them.

Ahead of us the glacier branches in two, and the flanks of Gasherbrum IV rise above the junction. We can now see most of it, but the summit remains in cloud. The junction is known as Concordia, and was named by the British mountaineer Martin Conway in 1892 after it reminded him of Konkordiaplatz, a junction on the Aletsch Glacier in Switzerland. The left branch leads north up the Godwin-Austen Glacier to K2, while the right branch heads south along the Upper Baltoro Glacier to Gasherbrum Base Camp, our destination. We will reach Concordia tomorrow morning. It's regarded as one of the world's great viewpoints, but I don't expect we'll see anything when we get there.

Phil has a laptop with him, and he's able to connect to the internet over a satellite connection. In the afternoon he comes to our tent to say he's just received an email from Michael Odell, one of our British friends. Michael has landed in Skardu, and is ready to trek out and join us; but our other friend, Mark Dickson, who was supposed to be with him, has had to stay in London due to work commitments.

We're surprised and disappointed for Mark. It's out of character for him to put work before mountaineering, and it was his idea that we all come to Gasherbrum this year. It was to be his fourth attempt at an 8,000m peak, and perhaps his best chance of climbing one. Phil says Mark is still talking to the airline, hoping to get another flight and join us when his work commitments have been resolved. But by the time he gets here, he'll be a long way behind us and running out of time if he wants to climb both G1 and G2.

In the mess tent later, Phil tells us about the last time he and Mark attempted Gasherbrum II, in 2007.

'Some Germans wrecked the mountain for us. We had shit weather for the trek in, like we're getting this time. When we got to Base Camp there was a lot more snow on the mountain than usual, and suddenly the weather was beautiful. Instead of waiting a couple of days for the snow to consolidate and stabilise, the Germans went up there anyway and caused an avalanche. Everyone went home after that. After the avalanche all the area between Camp 2 and Camp 3 was rock face, and it had become a rock climb. Nobody had come prepared for that. We needed anchors and pitons. None of us had brought any, so that was the climbing over.'

'It's actually mixed snow and ice, yeah?' Arian replies.

Phil shakes his head. 'No, it's normally just snow. It's straightforward. G2 was ruined, but if we had permits for G1 we still could have climbed that. That's why we've decided to do both of them this year.'

DAY 8
PORTER STRIKE

Thursday, 18 June 2009 – Gore II, Concordia Trek, Pakistan

It's snowing thickly again this morning, and this time we anticipate the porter strike that duly follows. We pack up our things in preparation for departure, but we leave the tents erect so that we can retreat inside if there's a delay.

There's a goat in the mess tent at breakfast. It's very quiet and still, and is standing on a box to keep its hooves warm. It's due to be our dinner when we get to Base Camp, but for the time being people can't resist stroking it amid predictable jokes about bringing their girlfriend with them on trek.

But the goat doesn't remain so well behaved. It tries to jump onto the dining table after we've left. When I return to the dining tent later in the morning, I discover that someone has tethered it to the tent poles with a leash so short that it can't stand up. There's a cut on one of its forelegs, and the ground is so cold that it prefers to stoop against its tether rather than lie down.

It's a pathetic sight. Although I'm due to eat it in a few days' time I can't help but feel sorry for it. I lay out the tent bags on the ground for it to lie on, and return to my tent to fetch a longer length of Prusik cord from my climbing kit. I give the goat a long enough leash to stand up comfortably, but short enough that it can't reach the table. The goat waits patiently while I fiddle with the rope around its horns, perhaps aware that I mean it no harm.

But shortly afterwards someone notices that it's been crapping on the floor of the dining tent. A member of our kitchen crew leads it away to lodge in one of the porter bivouacs. Poor goat. I can't imagine it will be treated with any sympathy there.

The snow continues throughout the morning. By noon it's clear we'll be going nowhere, and we settle down for another rest day. Phil brings us further bad news about Mark Dickson. He has a major business deal in the offing, and he needs to stay home to help close it. On top of this, he's been to the hospital for an X-ray. He twisted his ankle last month when he and I were descending from our ascent of Island Peak in Nepal. Mark being Mark, he shrugged it off and continued as if nothing happened, hoping it would heal. Clearly, it didn't.

'Now the idiot's discovered that it's broken in several places,' says Phil, who knows Mark well from an expedition here in 2007. 'He won't be joining us after all, but he wishes you guys luck.'

Ian and I are shocked. We can't believe our friend has missed out on another opportunity to climb an 8,000m peak. He has so much bad luck on big mountains.

'Sod's law we'll make it up both mountains now,' Phil says, 'and Mark'll be gutted.'

Our climbing team now comprises five Sherpas, leader Phil, and seven paying clients. We are very well supported, and I hope we don't blow it. We have so much time available that it will be really bad luck if the weather denies us.

One of the Sherpas, Serap Jangbu, is particularly determined. He has already climbed eleven of the fourteen mountains in the world over 8,000m. G1 and Broad Peak, which he'll be climbing with Philippe, would bring has tally to thirteen. He intends to return to Pakistan with a film crew next year to climb Nanga Parbat and complete the set. This would make him the first Nepali to climb all fourteen.

It's a much greater achievement for a Sherpa to accomplish this feat than a westerner, because Sherpas are never simply climbing for themselves. They have extra work to do fixing the route, carrying equipment up to the high camps for their clients, and breaking camp. Unlike westerners, Sherpas are rarely able to choose which mountains to climb. They have to take whatever work is offered.

Gore II is a very noisy campsite. Five expedition teams are waiting out the bad weather here, and several hundred porters huddle in camp. The murmur of voices is loud and constant, and there is human excrement all over the fringes of the camp.

To help pass the time later in the afternoon, Anna decides to start a snowball fight. She is surprised when about fifty porters respond to the challenge and eagerly pelt her.

DAY 9
CONCORDIA AND THE K2 CLEAN-UP PROJECT

Friday, 19 June 2009 – Shagring, Karakoram, Pakistan

We rise bleary eyed at 5.30, and obediently begin packing away our things. But today proves to be very different from yesterday, and we have reason to thank the striking porters.

I hear Phil's voice outside the tent.

'Mark, come outside. There's a great photo of Masherbrum.'

I hurriedly pull on my boots and climb out of the tent. The sky is completely clear and a shaft of golden sunlight is touching the north face of picturesque, pointed Masherbrum, rising above the Baltoro Glacier on its southern side.

It's one of those days when there are not enough superlatives to describe the scenery.

'It's the 19th,' Phil says. 'I've got to hand it to Jamie for calling it. He said the weather would improve on the 19th.'

Phil's business partner, Jamie McGuinness, has been sending him weather reports from Kathmandu. Several days ago Jamie said the weather would improve today. Assuming this wasn't a lucky guess, it's good to know that Phil is receiving reliable forecasts.

Arian and I are the last of our team to leave camp at 7.30. For the next three hours we amble up the Baltoro Glacier in the direction of Concordia. Every step is a photo opportunity, and our cameras are constantly out of their cases. The dusting of snow has covered the glacier moraine in a white carpet. To our left is the impressively steep Muztagh Tower, and behind us, to the right, the snow pyramid of Masherbrum. Up ahead of us the steep trapezoid of Gasherbrum IV dominates the skyline above Concordia. While the name 'Gasherbrum' has been variously translated from local languages as 'Beautiful Mountain' and 'Shining Wall', most people seem to agree that, of the seven Gasherbrums, it is to the distinctive Gasherbrum IV that the name originally refers.

As we approach Concordia, the massive dome of Broad Peak hovers into view, and to the right Mitre Peak pricks up like a needle. I arrive at Concordia, the junction of glaciers, at eleven o'clock. To the north, Broad Peak and the jagged outline of the much smaller Marble Peak stand as a gateway to the Godwin-Austen Glacier. Between them, at the end of the valley, the mighty K2 rises like a giant pyramid. From where I stand the Abruzzi Ridge forms its right-hand skyline. This is supposed to be the easiest route up, but it looks horribly steep. It's not a mountain I will ever be tempted to climb, but this is definitely in my top ten places to sit and have lunch.

K2 (8,611m) and Broad Peak (8,047m) from Concordia

There are lots of tents here, and as we are leaving, the Italian-funded Baltoro Glacier clean-up team invite Arian and I for tea. They will be spending five months cleaning all the camps between Askole and K2 Base Camp of detritus left by previous trekking and mountaineering parties. They are keen to tell us about their work, which involves not only litter picking, but a programme of education for porters and tour operators.

They have a display containing examples of some of the rubbish they've picked up this year. Empty gas canisters, beer tins, Coke cans and batteries can only have been left behind by tourists. Unfortunately, they're not allowed to clean up military waste. Our liaison officer, Major Iqbal, is sitting nearby and listening. He says that the military are the biggest polluters in the area, but have little sense of environmental responsibility. He seems embarrassed, and I admire his honesty in telling us.

For Arian the meeting is fortuitous. He is a student of environmental sciences at the University of Christchurch in New Zealand, and he is writing a master's dissertation on the highly specialised subject of waste management on 8,000m peaks in Pakistan. While the focus for the rest of us is getting to the summit of G2, Arian plans to clean up Camp 4. He says that tents and mountaineering waste have been abandoned there over the years, and if he doesn't act then nobody will ever bring it down.

He interviews the Baltoro clean-up team on camera. They offer to send porters to G2 Base Camp to take his rubbish back to Askole, where there is an incinerator. They say they will send copies of their reports – valuable data for his dissertation.

By the time we leave Concordia at one o'clock, we're a long way behind the rest of the team.

'Do you think Gordon will poke fun at us if we arrive in camp behind Bob?' Arian asks.

'He wouldn't be Gordon if he didn't.'

Concordia marks a junction for expedition teams. Trekkers and climbers to K2 and Broad Peak head north up the Godwin-Austen Glacier. Meanwhile those of us climbing the Gasherbrums branch south on the Upper Baltoro Glacier to

Gasherbrum Base Camp. Halfway between the latter and Concordia is Shagring Camp. I arrive there at 3.30. My late arrival means that the porters have already arrived, and my team mates have pitched the tents. Before retiring into mine, I have tea and biscuits in the dining tent with Phil, Philippe, Serap Jangbu and Tarke.

'Did you get to see K2,' Phil asks, 'or had it clouded over by then?'

'We had an amazing day,' I reply. 'We saw K2, Broad Peak and, apparently, G2 as well.'

David Hamilton, leader of the Jagged Globe G2 expedition, provided me with this information. There was a place on the approach to Concordia where several of the Gasherbrum peaks were visible in a line behind the more prominent G4. I know David from an expedition to Muztag Ata in China two years ago, and I bumped into his team at Concordia as we were passing through. He's something of an expert on the Karakoram, having led expeditions here many times. I felt sure G2 or G1 must be among the peaks we could see, so I asked him.

I describe the conversation I had with David to Phil and Serap Jangbu. They both insist the peak we saw was G1 rather than G2. This amuses me.

'Well, one of you superstar mountaineers must be wrong,' I say. 'Fat chance we have of reaching the summit if you can't even agree which mountain we're climbing.'

'What do you think?' says Philippe. 'Will either we or Jagged Globe end up climbing G3?'

Phil has been leaning hard against the table, and at this point he suddenly falls off his chair. The argument ends abruptly when I roar with laughter.

DAY 10
ARRIVAL AT BASE CAMP

Saturday, 20 June 2009 – Gasherbrum Base Camp, Pakistan

It's a short day today. We set off at 6.30am and continue up the
Upper Baltoro Glacier till it turns a corner to the left and
becomes the Abruzzi Glacier. Here Gasherbrum Base Camp sits
on a long finger of moraine at the foot of the South Gasherbrum
Glacier, a tumbling mass of ice, more like an icefall than a glacier.
Camp 1 lies in the Gasherbrum Cwm, 900m up the icefall. The
cwm is surrounded by the seven peaks of the Gasherbrum
group, and Phil says it's one of the most spectacular settings he
has ever been to.

From Base Camp, the main point of focus is Gasherbrum I,
the highest of them at 8,068m. Its south-west face rises 3,000m
above the icefall in a sheer wall of snow. The more I look at it, the
more I believe that I must be crazy to be thinking of climbing it.
Of course, all mountains have many facets. From the summit a
steep ridge leads down to the left. Our ascent route lies behind it
and hidden from view. Even so, I understand it to be extremely
steep. It will be the hardest peak I've ever attempted by some
margin, and only time will tell whether it will prove beyond me.

I reach Base Camp at 10.30. Serap Jangbu set off early to
reserve a location for us. He has chosen a spot right at the top
end of the moraine, as close as possible to the route through the
icefall. We spend the next couple of hours clearing snow away,

choosing and flattening pitches, and putting our tents up. In order to make Base Camp as comfortable as possible we have a tent each. I choose a pitch close to the edge of the icefall, angled in such a way that my front entrance looks straight up at G1. It's a great location, but it's cloudy this afternoon and I can see nothing of the mountain.

We're going to be here for the best part of two months, so it's important that we're happy. Gordon isn't quite so lucky with his choice of location. He has pitched his tent on top of a balcony of moraine. The expedition team below his lookout ask him to move because they're worried he will urinate in the snow outside his tent, which stands at the top of a snow slope they're using as their water source.

'Every time I step outside my tent, I see someone with binoculars looking up at me and checking I'm behaving myself,' he says.

Ian has spotted tracks in the snow outside his tent, possibly those of a pika, a tiny little rabbit-like mammal, the size of a mouse. It seems extraordinary that anything could live up here, thousands of metres above the vegetation zone, so I'm sure it can't be.

'Don't worry, Ian,' I tell him, 'the footprints are much too small to be a yeti.'

Gordon pinches Kate on the arm. 'Besides, they don't eat Englishmen. They'd far rather eat a nice juicy corn-fed American.'

I can't help thinking that she'd make a better meal than the tall, gangly Ian. I may not be the only one to have this thought, for everyone chuckles.

Shortly before lunch we say goodbye to most of our porters, who dump their loads and head straight back down the Baltoro Glacier to Askole. They have been a constant source of irritation to me, with their stopping and starting, their 'scuse me's' and their striking, but I know that I'm being ungracious. Accounts of early expeditions to the Karakoram are peppered with references to intense porter negotiations over load sizes and pay. We haven't had to worry about such details. We could just keep walking. We could never do this without their help. They have brought several tons of supplies up to Base Camp for us, but I certainly won't miss them now they're gone. It feels like a noisy town with 130 of them, and it will be so much more peaceful with just us and the kitchen crew.

DAY 11
THE VIEW FROM BASE CAMP

Sunday, 21 June 2009 – Gasherbrum Base Camp, Pakistan

It's the first time in over a week that we don't have to get up at the ungodly hour of 5.30. I savour my lie-in till eight o'clock, when breakfast is served – even though it's -5°C inside my tent. It's a crisp, clear morning and I have a great opportunity to take in our beautiful mountain surroundings.

From the summit of Gasherbrum I an easy snow ridge leads to the right, behind 7,069m Gasherbrum South. This is the route the Americans Andy Kauffman and Pete Schoening climbed when they made the first ascent of G1 in 1958. It's now out of bounds, and has been for many years since the Pakistan Army put a camp at its base, about half a mile away from us and close to the head of the Abruzzi Glacier.

Above the army camp the gently crevassed – though fiercely avalanche-prone – snow slopes of 7,424m Sia Kangri rise up close to the disputed borders of Pakistan, China and India. On its right flank is the Conway Saddle, dividing it from 7,312m Baltoro Kangri, also known as Golden Throne.

Beyond the Conway Saddle is another pass leading onto the vast Siachen Glacier. It is here that Pakistan and India meet head-to-head over disputed Kashmir, and the Siachen Glacier is sometimes referred to as the highest battleground in the world.

Baltoro Kangri rises directly above us on the opposite side of the Abruzzi Glacier. It's one of the closest mountains to Base Camp. Frequent avalanches tumble down its slopes and send a noisy rumble across the glacier to disturb our silence.

To its right sits the pointed snow triangle of 7,668m Chogolisa. It is here where the great Austrian mountaineer Hermann Buhl lost his life in 1957, just two weeks after completing the first ascent of Broad Peak. In front of Chogolisa, the Upper Baltoro Glacier vanishes round a corner to Concordia.

Immediately above Base Camp, and divided from Gasherbrum I by the South Gasherbrum Icefall, is 7,004m Gasherbrum VI, the second smallest of the Gasherbrum Group. From camp it looks like a brown rock trapezium crowned by a steep snow crest.

Today is a lazy rest day. In the morning I sort out my climbing kit. I have some new anti-balling plates to fit to my crampons, to prevent snow building up on my feet and rendering the crampons useless. I discover that I've bought the wrong plates, and I have to improvise a solution. This involves chopping my old plates in half, keeping the toe end, and fitting the new heel ends and rubber concertina to the central bar of the crampons. I hope this will work in the short term and last the expedition, but eventually the toe ends of my old rubber plates will disintegrate, just like the heels. I also insert new insoles into my mountaineering boots. In Nepal last month the boots ripped the skin off my heels as I was climbing Mera Peak, and it was uncomfortable to climb in them. I still need to find a sock solution that will stop this happening again, and I hope the moulded insoles from my other boots will help.

I spend the remainder of the afternoon lying in my tent, reading my book. Every so often I get some exercise by going to the dining tent to fill up my mug with copious quantities coffee, and walking across the moraine to pee.

Tarke tells me off for emptying my pee bottle outside my tent on the wrong side of camp. One side of the moraine has been designated the peeing side, while the other side is where snow and ice are gathered for drinking water. My tent is upstream from the rest of camp, but a good fifty metres above the next campsite down. By the time my pee has soaked through the moraine, then frozen, merged with the ice below, and slowly moved down the valley at a few inches a day by the Abruzzi Glacier, the team in the neighbouring campsite will have long since packed up and gone. The chances of somebody digging out my undiluted pee in future years seem fairly remote. But camp rules are camp rules, and from now on I obediently cross the campsite to empty my bladder.

DAY 12
PUJA

Monday, 22 June 2009 – Gasherbrum Base Camp, Pakistan

It's another beautiful morning, and I wonder how long the good weather will last. At breakfast Phil outlines our plans for the day. By tradition the Sherpas won't put foot on any big mountain before they've conducted a puja, or blessing ceremony, for our success and safety on the climb.

'It's rubbish really,' Phil says, as sympathetic as always, 'but if we bring five superstar Sherpas with us to help climb the mountain, we've got to let them have their way. After the puja, anyone who wants to can put their climbing kit on and we'll head up onto the ice for a couple of hours.'

The puja is due to take place at nine o'clock, which means we probably won't get started till ten. By this time the sun will be high and warming the ice, increasing the risk of collapsing serac towers in the icefall.

'Will the icefall be safe that late in the morning?' I ask Phil.

'Icefall? This ain't a goddamn icefall, buddy. This is a snowdrift.'

If I wanted an intelligent answer, then I should have asked someone else.

I smile. It reminds me of a conversation I overheard between Phil and Arian a couple of days ago. They were talking about Diamox, a drug that is often used at high altitude to help people acclimatise.

'Is Diamox safe, Phil?' Arian asked.

'What do mean is it safe?' Phil replied. 'Do you think it's going to give you herpes or something? Of course it's safe.'

In the absence of a lama, or Buddhist monk, Serap Jangbu conducts the puja for us. The Sherpas have erected a cairn with a flagpole at the highest point among the moraine ridges of our campsite. We've piled our ice axes and crampons around it, and the Sherpas have placed various foodstuffs, such as potatoes, cereal and Tibetan bread.

For about ten minutes Serap kneels in front of the cairn and chants while the rest of us sit behind in a wide arc. When he finishes chanting, the other Sherpas unroll prayer flags from the flagpole and extend them outwards. They attach them to smaller cairns around the campsite, like the spokes of a wheel. We are given handfuls of rice and tsampa, which we toss into the air with a cry of *lagyelo*, which means 'victory to the gods' in Tibetan. This is to acknowledge that the fate of our expedition – whether we reach the summits or merely survive to climb another day – is in the hands of the mountain gods.

Whether it's rubbish or not, one thing is certain. We're more likely to succeed with a happy and confident Sherpa team, so the puja serves a useful purpose.

Our short walk into the icefield fills me with anticipation for the weeks ahead of us. We weave around and over crevasses and seracs, beneath the feet of Gasherbrum I. We gradually turn a corner which brings Gasherbrum II into view. We can see all the route above Camp 2. It climbs a snow shoulder, then passes in front of a prominent triangular rock face that forms the summit pyramid. The final climb to the summit is up the right-hand side of the triangle.

At eleven o'clock we turn around and head back down before we get too deep into the serac towers of the icefall. It's late to be in here, and the trail we've followed is already turning to slush. The route has been well tramped already, though, and this has helped. We had been half-expecting to spend a few days' enforced rest at Base Camp while our Sherpas looked for a route through the icefall to Camp 1. But now we see that somebody has done this already, and marked the trail with bamboo wands. This has saved us several days.

Ascending the icefall with Gasherbrum I up ahead

Back at Base Camp for lunch, Phil hands out some of his mountaineering tips.

'Make sure you don't leave food in your tent porch at any of the higher camps. The crows here are a menace and will sniff it out, ripping through the side of the tent if necessary. If you're leaving any sleeping bags and shit up at Camp 1 when you're down in Base Camp for some rest, make sure you put them back in their stuff sacks and tie everything together in a bundle. If there's a storm on the mountain that destroys the tents, a single sleeping bag unrolled is much more likely to end up in China.'

DAY 13
A PARTING AND A WELCOME

Tuesday, 23 June 2009 – Gasherbrum Base Camp, Pakistan

It's another clear morning. The good weather seems to be holding, but there is a large plume of cloud rising off the summit of Gasherbrum I, indicating strong winds. Gorgan walks into the dining tent and gives us his opinion about the climbing conditions.

'I think if this was your summit day on G1 you would have to go for it. That's why you need a big dick.'

I'm not sure I agree that these are suitable conditions for launching a summit attempt on G1, but by his criteria I'd be stuffed anyway.

After breakfast we say goodbye to our trekkers, Bob, Anna and Kate, who head back down the Baltoro Glacier the same way we came. They will be back in Askole in five days' time. We also say goodbye to our liaison officer, Major Iqbal of the Pakistan Army, who goes with them. He has been a thoroughly nice chap, and I will remember our conversations about cricket fondly. From now on, we are just climbers.

After lunch we're joined by the final member of our party, Michael Odell. Despite leaving the UK more than a week later than us, he has been lucky with flights and made good time on the trail. He has arrived in Base Camp just three days after us.

Ian and I pitch his tent while Ashad, our cook, brews him tea.

39

Afterwards we sit in the dining tent talking about our mutual friend, Mark Dickson, who is no longer joining the expedition after breaking his ankle in Nepal last month.

'Well, he tells us he's broken his ankle,' Michael says, 'but maybe he's having second thoughts about spending two months in a country where there's no alcohol.'

This was going to be Mark's fourth attempt at an 8,000m peak.

'I'm sure he'll climb an 8,000er one day,' Ian says.

'Yeah. There will be a cable car or a stairlift up K2 by then,' Phil says.

Later in the afternoon Ian and I wander over to the camp of one of our neighbours, Jagged Globe. We know several of their team members, leaders and guides, and they are very welcoming. They even give us some real filter coffee. They claim to have supplies of booze, but I'm not sure if this is a wind-up.

'You're a rival team, so if you fall down a crevasse we'll not try and rescue you,' says their leader David Hamilton, with whom I climbed Muztag Ata in China a couple of years ago. 'Instead we'll dangle a bottle of whiskey on a rope to annoy you.'

I laugh. 'That's fine. In Ian's case there's no better way of getting him out.'

DAY 14
UP TO CAMP 1

Wednesday, 24 June 2009 – Camp 1, Gasherbrum Cwm

Today is our first walk through the icefall of the South Gasherbrum Glacier to Camp 1. Arian wants to leave in the middle of the night, at three o'clock; but Tarke the superstar says it's much too early. We agree to leave at five.

Although there was snow last night, the fine weather is holding, and we wake up to still winds. It has stopped snowing too. Thanks to the later start, the pressure is on to get through the icefall before the sun gets too high and starts melting the seracs and snow bridges.

I share a rope with Phil and Ian. They're miles quicker than I am. The climb to Camp 1 is supposed to take up to eight hours, but Phil, who leads our rope, manages to get us there in just six. As we weave between seracs and crevasses, Gasherbrums II, III and IV all pop into view one by one, and the scenery is stunning. But I concentrate on putting one foot in front of the other and mouthing obscenities as I struggle towards the top of the climb.

We reach Camp 1, beneath the south face of Gasherbrum II, at eleven o'clock. Our Sherpa team have already erected the tents. I'm absolutely exhausted, and I lie down in the snow in front of our camp doing my Darth Vader impression. It's about an hour before I'm breathing normally again. The others all seem to be fine, which is a good sign – for them, at least.

I'm blessed to be sharing a tent with Ian. He's quite happy to brew up copious amounts of coffee while I recover. I unpack my Therm-a-Rest, sleeping bag and the food that I've carried up, then spend most of the afternoon crashed out. I do manage a short foray outside to admire the view, which is one of the most spectacular I've ever seen.

Phil crouches with Gasherbrums III and II behind

The Gasherbrum Cwm is a high horseshoe surrounded by the seven Gasherbrum peaks. These range between 7,000 and 8,000 metres in height. Every single one of them is spectacular. Our first objective, G2, now rises a little over 2,000m above us. The first half looks daunting, up a steep snow ridge, though the final summit section looks a little easier. Thankfully we have our fantastic Sherpa team with us, who head up towards Camp 2 in the afternoon to fix the route with ropes while we vegetate in our tents.

DAY 15
AN UNUSUAL CASE OF FROSTBITE

Thursday, 25 June 2009 – Gasherbrum Base Camp, Pakistan

I wake up at five o'clock with a bit of a headache, probably due to dehydration rather than altitude. Camp 1 is at 5,910m. As well as spending several nights at 5,000m already, I've been higher than this in the last month and a half while climbing in Nepal. I should therefore be quite well acclimatised.

Rather than waking up an hour earlier to begin the time-consuming process of boiling water for breakfast, we agreed last night that we'd simply wake up this morning, pack our things and descend straight back to Base Camp for breakfast. Even if we'd wanted to cook this morning, we may not have been able to. We left the gas canister in the porch of our tent overnight, and it's probably too frozen to fire up.

We leave Camp 1 at six o'clock, and the descent takes just two and a half hours. Going down is easy, but I'd forgotten how much undulation there was over the ridges and folds of the icefall just above Base Camp. It's frustrating having to do so much climbing when I'm still tired after yesterday. I keep feeling the rope slacken behind me, and I can tell Ian's itching to descend faster. It's a relief that Phil, in front, isn't influenced by this, and he keeps up a regular pace all the way down.

Back at Base Camp, our kitchen crew of Ashad, Ehshan and Shezad have waited for our arrival before preparing breakfast.

It's good to demolish some eggs and chapatis after the freeze-dried food and snacks we've been nibbling on at Camp 1.

At lunch Arian tells an awkward story about Ali, an Iranian climber who trekked in with us from Askole.

'I passed him yesterday on the way up to Camp 1 and asked how he was. "I don't feel so good," he said, pointing to his abdomen. "You have stomach ache?" I asked, but he pointed lower down. Eventually I realised he was pointing at his dick, and he said it was frozen.'

Most people around the table are laughing, but a few of us wince. I find the story hard to credit.

'How on earth did he manage to do that?' I ask. 'I've heard of frostbite in the fingers and toes, but never in the penis. Surely it doesn't get cold enough for that?'

I look at Phil. If anyone's heard of other cases of frozen members it's likely to be him.

'Dude, on Denali it's so cold you have to pee through a sock,' he replies.

'How cold?'

'Minus fifty. It's easily cold enough to freeze your dick off having a piss.'

It's not anything like that cold here. Last night in the tent at Camp 1, the temperature didn't get below -15°C.

'Surely you can't get frostbite having a piss here,' I persist. 'You're not exposed for long enough.'

This choice of phrase raises a few chuckles.

Phil agrees. 'Ali G's been doing something perverted, that's for sure.'

We task Arian, our base camp networker, with finding out how Ali obtained his unfortunate injury.

Just before dinner, Gombu, Pasang and Temba return from their rope fixing above Camp 1. The route is now fixed all the way to Camp 2. Our Sherpas shared the workload with the Pakistani high-altitude porters (HAPs) on the Jagged Globe team.

Although our sirdar, Gombu, was keen to fix the route all the way to Camp 3, David Hamilton, leader of the Jagged Globe expedition, wants to ask other teams in Base Camp for contributions before fixing any more of the route. He believes they will all use our ropes, and he wants to charge them $300 a head. If nobody pays, then our teams will fix the ropes just before we need them, and take them down again afterwards.

This may sound mercenary, but it's normal practice on busier mountains. Our teams have paid more to bring extra rope and resources in the form of HAPs and Sherpas. In any case, there is another consideration behind the decision. If the route to Camp 3 is fixed too early, fresh snowfall could bury the ropes before we get round to using them. When the new snow becomes frozen it will be hard work to dig them out again.

DAY 16
MY BLEEDING ANKLES

Friday, 26 June 2009 – Gasherbrum Base Camp, Pakistan

We have a full day's rest at Base Camp today. I spend most of the morning reading in my tent.

I'm concerned about the wound on my left ankle, caused by my boots rubbing. One layer of skin has peeled off completely, and the boot began rubbing on the second layer as I came down yesterday. If two layers of skin get pulled off every time I wear the boots, it's clear that I will run out of feet long before the expedition is over. I dress the wound and hobble around on the moraine outside my tent, trying to figure out how to make the boots more comfortable. The right boot was rubbing in Nepal last month and now seems to be OK, but the left boot continues to be a problem. If I can't fix it I'll just have to climb through the pain, but my ill-fitting boots remain my biggest concern.

Phil says he will let the Sherpas decide when we go back up the mountain. On our next foray we will climb to Camp 2 and spend the night there before returning to Base Camp to rest. We need the Sherpas to establish the camp for us, and it's important they're well rested before they go back up again.

When he was told he couldn't fix the route to Camp 3, a bored Gombu, our sirdar and ultimate decision-maker for the Sherpa team, spent the afternoon digging a posh toilet in the snow at Camp 1. This morning I hear shouts and laughter outside my tent and peer out to see all five of them dragging a barrel of glacier water up the ice slope beside our camp. They do this three times to provide our kitchen crew with plenty of water for cooking, and seem to be enjoying themselves. So much for letting them rest.

In the afternoon, I play cards in the dining tent with Gorgan, Gordon and Michael. Phil enters to say they've decided to take another rest day tomorrow. We'll set off up the mountain again on Sunday. Although he only arrived in Base Camp three days ago, Michael says he will come with us, which means he will be back on the same climbing schedule. Providing he is sufficiently acclimatised, this shouldn't be a problem. He's a good deal younger and fitter than most of us.

DAY 17
BASE CAMP POLITICS

Saturday, 27 June 2009 – Gasherbrum Base Camp, Pakistan

Another day of patiently waiting down in Base Camp, and another day of fine weather. It surely can't last. We've received news that a weather front will arrive across the Karakoram on July 1st. This will give us time to make another foray up the mountain, to Camp 2 this time, before returning to Base Camp to sit out any bad weather it may bring. We will need to make a night start tonight. Given what happened last time, the majority of the team are in favour of an earlier three o'clock start up the icefall.

I pass the time today reading, doing some washing, and playing cards in the dining tent with Ian, Michael, Arian and Gordon. Base Camp politics interrupt our game when a small Canadian group arrives and tries to pitch their tents on the moraine just below us. Our cook, Ashad, witnesses the argument that follows.

'I give you fuckers five minutes to move your fucking tents,' a member of the international team they have tried to camp beside says.

This is the same team, containing members from the UK, Canada, New Zealand, Sweden and Brazil, who complained that Gordon's tent was too close to their water source. They intend to climb the less popular mountains G3 and G4, and the feeling around Base Camp is that there is an element of snobbery at play. They feel different from the rest of us. We are here with commercial groups to climb the 'easier' peaks of G1 and G2 in a supported fashion. By contrast they are true alpinists, climbing in a purer style. This may be true, but it all seems very petty. This is only a narrow section of moraine on a glacier, and no expedition team can claim ownership of any particular patch.

Gasherbrums IV (7,925m), III (7,952m) and II (8,035m) seen from the bottom of the icefall

The new arrivals, from a company called Canada West, come and ask Phil if they can camp beside us. They're only a small team with two clients, a leader and a couple of high-altitude porters, and Phil is more than happy. We're expecting a huge group of twenty Iranian climbers to arrive any day, who will need to find a space in Base Camp alongside the rest of us. We would rather have this much smaller team camping next to us. Even so, the Canadian team still has to trudge up to the army camp beyond us to obtain permission from the Pakistan Army before they can camp here.

On a sorrier note, a spot of stomach trouble and a frozen

penis has meant that Ali, the Iranian who trekked in with us, has decided to go home after just seven days at Base Camp. He has climbed no higher than Camp 1. We're all very sorry for him. When the survival of one's frozen member is at stake, it is always good to remember that the mountain will still be here next year – while the appendage may not.

I'm sure Ali has made the right decision.

DAY 18
EXHAUSTED AGAIN

Sunday, 28 June 2009 – Camp 1, Gasherbrum Cwm, Pakistan

At 1.30am I hear snow pattering on the roof of my tent, but by two o'clock it's finished. This is good news. If the weather forecast is correct, and there's a storm coming over on July 1st, we can't afford another rest day at Base Camp if we're to make our foray up to Camp 2 and get back down again before it strikes.

By three o'clock, seven of us are on our way back up the icefall: me, Ian, Phil, Michael, Arian, Gordon and Tarke. The temperature is mild, surprisingly so, and this causes problems in the early part of the climb. Streams of meltwater are flowing off the glacier. Phil puts his foot through thin ice into one of them, and ends up freezing his leg. Crevasses are widening and snow bridges are melting. There's a high chance of ending up in a crevasse, and I'm glad Phil is in front – not because I want him to fall in one, but because he has less chance of doing so than novices like me.

We start unroped because the route is extremely fiddly up and down pressure ridges and around seracs. Phil nearly goes through a snow bridge, and Ian and I have to hold on to him while he diverts around a yawning crevasse. Later, when we are roped, I have to do the same – I try to leap a crevasse, and the snow on the other side gives way beneath me as I jump onto it. I manage to recover by throwing myself forwards, and I prod away with my ice axe to find an alternative safe route around. On another occasion my right leg disappears a metre into deep snow, and in yanking it out I pull the crampon off my boot. Fortunately Michael is walking behind me and he sees what has happened. He shouts to alert me, and I stop to put it on again before I walk any distance cramponless.

All this happens during darkness, under the light of our head torches. Phil rushes us deliberately. It's more dangerous than normal, and the rapid pace, coupled with no stops to rest mean that for a second time in succession I'm exhausted before the climb has really got going. If I have to maintain this pace on summit day then it's going to kill me.

Once through the more intensively crevassed section at the bottom of the icefall, the remainder of the climb is straightforward. We reach Camp 1 at eight o'clock. This time it has taken us just five hours.

For a reason I never quite understand, most of my crazy companions decide to continue to Camp 2 today. I'm more than happy to extend my acclimatisation by spending a night here and continuing to Camp 2 tomorrow. Michael also stays at Camp 1 because he's spent less time at high altitude than we have. Tarke remains to keep us company.

It's become clear that I'm the least fit member of the team. I believe I'm capable of climbing this mountain if I can take things easier and complete the climb at my own pace. But the question is whether the others will let me do that.

They set off for Camp 2 at nine o'clock. Shortly afterwards it begins to snow, but at 11.30 a break in the cloud allows us to see four tiny figures on a feature called the Banana Ridge, high on the snow face. It looks horribly steep, but we are looking at the route head on.

We give the matter no further thought and fall asleep for a couple of hours. When I wake up, the sun is pounding on the tent and it's sweltering inside. I go out to have another look across the Gasherbrum Cwm. It's one of the most amazing mountain settings anywhere, surrounded by six Gasherbrum peaks, each one of them glittering and majestic. The afternoon is restful as we listen to avalanches blasting the slopes of this amphitheatre.

In the evening we cook one of those disgusting backpacker meals that involve adding water to a packet of freeze-dried ingredients and letting it simmer. This time we have some sort of Thai noodle soup. I pour a fairly watery soup into Michael's mug, but when I come to pour mine, a fist-sized chunk of glued-together noodle lands in my mug. There's clearly a technique to cooking these meals I haven't grasped yet. Neither of us finds the food at all tasty, and we bury what we're unable to finish under snow in the porch of our tent. We make a pact not to tell Arian the environmental warrior.

DAY 19
CAMP 2 AND THE BANANA RIDGE

Monday, 29 June 2009 – Camp 2, Gasherbrum II, Pakistan

Undeterred by last night's culinary disaster, Michael and I wake at five o'clock to boil water for breakfast. We decide to have a backpacker breakfast of granola with bananas and milk. It's the same cooking method as yesterday – pour hot water into the mix and stir it up – but this time it's actually quite nice. I'm gobsmacked, but I suppose there's less either we or the manufacturers can do wrong with breakfast cereal.

Michael, Tarke and I set off for Camp 2 and the fabled Banana Ridge at seven o'clock. It depressed me looking at this feature yesterday afternoon as we watched figures hardly moving on what looked like an almost sheer snow face.

In the end it doesn't turn out to be too bad. A short walk across flat snow brings us to the point where Gasherbrum II rises abruptly above the Gasherbrum Cwm. The climb begins with a gentle zigzag up steep snow, and for once I don't find myself trying to keep up with a crazy pace. Tarke leads with a comfortable plod, stopping frequently for us to take a few deep breaths.

When we get to the start of the fixed ropes, we don't consider the first section steep enough to warrant jumars. We clip in with our safety carabiners and continue plodding up slowly. About halfway up, the trail passes to the right underneath an ice cliff, and then to the left back over it. The sky is completely clear and we have great views of all the mountains surrounding the Cwm, most notably Gasherbrum I and Gasherbrum II above us.

Just before we reach the Banana Ridge, we meet Phil, Gordon, Arian and Ian coming back down.

'Man, they were fucked yesterday afternoon,' Phil says, arriving ahead of the others. 'Gordon fucked; Ian fucked.'

'So they were all fucked – does that mean we can switch to a more sensible schedule for our summit push?' I ask. 'Base Camp to Camp 1, 1 to 2, 2 to 3, and then the summit.'

Phil nods. 'It's looking like it, dude. Just 'cos I decided to go all the way up to Camp 2 myself, it didn't mean the others had to follow me.'

This is a relief. Back in Base Camp a couple of days ago someone asked whether we'd be skipping Camp 1 on our summit push, like the others did yesterday. Phil said if you can't go straight from Base Camp to Camp 2 in a single push then you shouldn't be on the mountain.

He has far greater experience than I do, but I can't help thinking there is another important consideration. The main purpose of the days prior to summit day is to ensure you're rested enough and acclimatised enough to be in the best possible shape for the summit dash. By climbing 1,350m from Base Camp to Camp 2, followed by 800m from Camp 2 to Camp 3, it doesn't seem like you're going to be in optimal shape for a 900m summit day above 7,000m straight afterwards.

I believe I'm capable of climbing this mountain, but the biggest risk is exhausting myself by being forced into the punishing pace and schedule the others are setting themselves. I wouldn't like to say 'I told you so' or be pleased that my companions arrived at Camp 2 yesterday 'fucked' (if I may use Phil's terminology), but I think their push straight from Base Camp to Camp 2 was completely pointless. Michael and I have had two comfortable days' climbing with plenty of rest. We've had an extra night at 5,900m to help us acclimatise. The weather has been an added bonus: instead of climbing in a snow storm like they did yesterday, we have perfect skies and have stopped frequently for photos.

The Banana Ridge curves gradually to the left and climbs 200m to the campsite behind a prominent rock buttress that we could see from Camp 1. There is a short drop into camp, and we arrive there shortly after 10.30, after just 3½ hours' climbing. I don't need to remind myself that Ian, normally much quicker than me, took five hours and arrived... well, quite tired. But I do anyway.

Climbing the Banana Ridge

The rock buttress hides most of the Gasherbrum Cwm, but Gasherbrum I is still visible across the Gasherbrum La, and G2's summit is now much closer above us.

We're at 6,420m, and this morning's ascent has made me feel much better about the whole climb. We've made it up the steepest feature on the mountain with no real difficulty. Tarke's pace today has been just right, and I've had the first intimation from Phil that my slower pace and desire for shorter days can be accommodated. He may even recommend it to some of the others. I also seem to be acclimatising well and am sleeping decently at high camps – so far – though for tonight we will have to see.

Michael seems to be a bit under the weather this afternoon, though. He enjoyed the climb and got plenty of liquid down him when we arrived in camp, but since lying down to rest he has picked up a severe headache. This is probably as a result of his shorter acclimatisation schedule. We go back to Base Camp tomorrow morning, and a storm is forecast, so he will have plenty of time to recover.

I prepare coffee, soup and chicken casserole for dinner, but the soup is too much for Michael. He has to crawl outside the tent to throw it back up again. I put this down to his lack of acclimatisation, rather than my cookery skills. During our six o'clock radio call to Base Camp Phil confirms this by recommending a Diamox to help him recover, rather than something more drastic to flush his system out, like an enema.

DAY 20
BLIZZARD ON THE BANANA RIDGE

Tuesday, 30 June 2009 – Gasherbrum Base Camp, Pakistan

It's snowing when I wake up this morning. We know that a storm is on the way. We have to get down from Camp 2 to Base Camp for a few days' rest, and to wait out the bad weather. It's -9°C in the tent when I wake up, and my fingers are cold as I perform the morning routine of putting on my harness and crampons. I know ropework is required this morning, so I put on my thinner gloves that allow me some manual dexterity, rather than my nice warm down mitts.

At 7.45, while Tarke is collapsing the tents at Camp 2 and marking them with bamboo wands in preparation for the storm which is sure to bury them, I plod up the short snow slope that leads to Camp 2. At the top of the slope is a narrow ridge leading to the rock buttress overlooking the top of the Banana Ridge. This morning the horizontal ridge is barely discernible among the sea of white that envelops my vision. Fresh snow has obliterated the footprints of yesterday, and all I have to guide me along it is the thin dark line of fixed rope, which I clip onto with my safety carabiner. Although this will be sufficient to protect me in the event of a slip, I have no wish to find myself dangling in my harness above the 500m drop to the Gasherbrum Cwm on either side of me. I nudge my way along it, making certain every step I take lands on a bed of solid snow.

After two rope lengths I reach the top of the Banana Ridge and look down it. This is where the serious climbing starts, and I'm going to have to descend this formidable 200m feature in a howling blizzard.

I begin by facing outwards, looking down the ridge and carefully descending yesterday's steps. I clutch the fixed rope with one hand, and use the prong of my ice axe to dig into the snow with the other. The steps are disappearing fast, and as fresh snow slides beneath my feet it quickly becomes clear this is not a safe way to descend. I turn around and face towards the slope. I now have a third point of contact with the mountain as I look down, searching for the remains of steps. I carefully lower myself using the front points of my crampons to dig into the snow.

My only safety precaution beyond these three points of contact – my crampons, my ice axe, and my gloved hand on the fixed rope – is a carabiner clipped onto the fixed rope and attached to my harness. Although this will save my life by preventing me tumbling 500m to the Gasherbrum Cwm, I will still fall all the way down to the next anchor point. This could be an entire rope length if I happen to be at the top of one when I slip. It would certainly put the willies up me for the rest of the descent, and I'm determined not to let it happen.

I make painstaking progress. My fingers become numb with cold, causing my grip on the fixed rope to weaken. As drifting snow howls across my face, I know I have to forget about the cold and the slow progress, and continue down step by step. It will take as long as it takes, and there's little I can do about it.

I've descended a little more than one rope length when I notice Tarke and Michael appear at the top of the Banana Ridge above me and begin following me down. The front-pointing is tiring on my calves; every so often, when I reach a step big enough to accommodate my whole foot, I stop and rest. Then I hear Tarke shout something down to me. I look up and Michael repeats the instruction.

'Mark, try abseiling.'

Until now I'd believed fixed ropes to be too tight to abseil off, but I see Michael descending quickly towards me. I reach behind my back to unclip my figure-of-eight loop from my harness. I'm at the top of the third fixed rope, but when I try to snatch a bight out of it to attach the figure-of-eight I find it too tight and struggle to grab enough.

Michael is much closer to me now, and I resume front-pointing, but this time much more quickly, almost recklessly. After I've descended another ten metres I look down the ridge and see how much farther I have to descend in this painstaking fashion. It's disheartening and it feels like it's going to take hours. I try to attach the abseil device again. This time the weight of my descent on the fixed rope has stretched it a little, and I'm able to attach the device without difficulty. This is a massive relief – not only is abseiling much quicker, but also much safer and less tiring as I lean back and let the rope slip through my figure-of-eight loop.

It takes ten to twelve abseils to reach the bottom of the Banana Ridge, but now I can enjoy myself. When I turn the corner to reach its base, and wait for Tarke and Michael to catch up, I even find my fingers have warmed up again.

From here, we have a straightforward if frustrating descent to Camp 1. A few inches of fresh snow cover the route, obliterating most of the old tracks and making for a tedious descent. Ending up on my backside in the snow is a constant hazard. As the snow continues to fall we pass a lone nutcase on his way up. With a storm forecast it seems inevitable he will be stranded at Camp 2 in dangerous conditions for several days. Hopefully he will reach the Banana Ridge, look up it, and have the good sense to turn around.

At last we reach the bottom of the face and trudge across the Gasherbrum Cwm to Camp 1. Here we pause only to drop off our sleeping bags and mats before roping up and continuing our descent.

It's 10.20am when we leave. This time our descent to Base Camp is slower. The wind continues to blow spindrift across our faces. The low temperatures ensure snow bridges and ice towers in the South Gasherbrum Icefall remain intact, but fresh snow begins to cover old tracks and brings the new risk of hidden crevasses.

The bottom section of the icefall is a dispiriting obstacle for tired feet. There are almost as many ascents as descents, with plenty of snow ridges and ice seracs to climb over. The snow becomes slushy towards the bottom, and my crampons ball up with fresh snow. I have to keep asking Tarke and Michael to stop so that I can bash the snow off with my ice axe.

As we approach Base Camp, Michael has a more serious problem. He looks down at his feet and notices one of his crampons has disappeared. I was behind him on the rope, and I didn't notice it fall off, but I do remember seeing a single crampon lying in the snow as we passed through another campsite that a newly arrived group of Iranian climbers were pitching on the moraine beyond ours. Michael rushes back and is relieved to discover it was his. A missing crampon would have meant the end of his expedition.

We stay roped up all the way down and are tired when we trudge into the safety of Base Camp at 1.30pm. Ehshan, one of the kitchen assistants, brings over a pot of orange juice, and in the dining tent we find a sweet and sour meat dish with rice ready for us. It's music to my ears when Phil tells us we now have four or five days of rest at Base Camp before our summit push.

DAY 21
DAY ONE OF DOING NOTHING

Wednesday, 1 July 2009 – Gasherbrum Base Camp, Pakistan

Day one of doing nothing, and for most of the day it's easy. As I lie in my tent and listen to the snow pounding on the roof, it's clear nobody's going anywhere for a while.

I finish reading my book – *Shogun*, all 1,243 pages – and am glad of it. It's full of death – victims having their heads chopped off with samurai swords, or people committing suicide by slicing their bellies open and watching the entrails spill out onto the floor. I prefer books with sympathetic, likeable characters, and I'm looking forward to returning to my classics.

At about five o'clock in the afternoon, after it has snowed non-stop all day, the sun finally emerges from the gloom. We all escape from our tents to look out upon a fantastic winter mountain scene.

Michael grabs the chance to take down his tent and re-erect it on a flatter platform. Phil is absolutely delighted with the change in the weather. His attempts to charge his big battery with solar panels have become a comical Keystone Kops-style theme over the last week. I ask him to explain the various electrical gadgets that support the expedition – the radio base station, the battery and the Thuraya satellite connection – while I shoot a video. Unfortunately Gordon ruins it by looking over my shoulder and asking if he can spy an anal vibrator in the corner of Phil's tent.

Several of us take the opportunity to photograph this changed landscape. Since the whole team is here in one place for the first time in a few days, we have a group photo on the puja platform, with Gasherbrum I in the background.

DAY 22
TEA WITH THE MOUNTAINEERING ELITE

Thursday, 2 July 2009 – Gasherbrum Base Camp, Pakistan

Day two of doing nothing. The weather is mostly fine, but avalanche risk means we can't go up the mountain until the newly fallen snow has consolidated.

After washing some clothes, I go for a wander up the moraine finger beyond the army camp with Ian and Michael. Our aim is to get a view of Gasherbrum II, which can't be seen from our camp on the moraine. Although it's predominantly sunny today, a veil of mist in the Gasherbrum Cwm obscures most of the mountains, including G2.

Back in my tent it's absolutely sweltering. I try to read some of my latest book, *Tom Jones*, but it's uncomfortably hot, so I spend most of the afternoon in the dining tent playing cards with Gordon, Gorgan, Ian and Michael. After Gordon spots me taking a sneaky peek at Gorgan's cards they all try to stitch me up. Somehow they fail, and I still manage to win the game, enhancing the erroneous reputation of being a card genius that I acquired earlier in the trip.

The Finnish mountaineer Veikka Gustafsson and Jagged Globe leader David Hamilton join us for afternoon tea. Veikka is here to climb Gasherbrum I, and if he is successful it will be his fourteenth and final 8,000m peak. This would put him into a select group of less than twenty climbers.

We discuss the various conflicting weather forecasts available to us. The popular consensus is that there may be one or two fine days ahead of us, but a lot of new snow arriving on the 6th, followed by clear weather. G2 is dangerously avalanche prone above Camp 2 after new snow. Phil knows this only too well after he watched a group of German mountaineers trigger an avalanche there two years ago. The avalanche killed two members of the German team, and it changed the terrain so significantly that it effectively closed the mountain. There doesn't seem to be much point in budging from Base Camp until the 7th at the earliest.

'But that still means we could potentially summit on the 10th or 11th,' Phil says. 'We could go straight from Base Camp to Camp 2 like we did the other day. You were all strong enough to manage it.'

I don't know whether he's trying to show off to Veikka or David, but there are a few smirks around the table. Before any of us say anything he qualifies his statement.

'Actually we did it, but everyone was…'

'Yes, we were quite tired weren't we, Phil,' I say.

We talk about the possibility of getting the route fixed on G1 – a steeper mountain, less avalanche prone – while we wait for a weather window on G2. David and Phil have met with other groups at Base Camp to get contributions for the rope fixing. Some of these contributions have come in the form of rope, and Phil now thinks they have enough to fix virtually the whole of G1.

David has reached the summit of G1 before, and Veikka has been within fifty metres of it, so they discuss options. Veikka doesn't need the fixed ropes, but it seems he may be happy to wait for our Sherpas to break trail (I guess you don't climb all the 8,000m peaks without knowing how to conserve your energy). Serap Jangbu is equally keen to get up there to complete one of his three remaining 8,000m peaks.

One of David's team members called Paul has decided to go home because he's frustrated by their lack of progress on G2. It's a surprise because he's their strongest climber, and has already summited Everest. They still have plenty of time left, and when the weather closes in there's no alternative but to be patient and wait at Base Camp for a summit opportunity.

He's not the only person to leave early, as Phil reminds us.

'And Ali's gone home because of his frozen dick,' he says.

This has been a common talking point, and always draws hoots of laughter every time it's mentioned. Poor Ali.

'Ah, but that's a good reason for going home,' I reply.

We're still not sure if the story is really true, but Arian, our source, insists it's what Ali told him.

'But you never found out how he did it,' Gordon says.

'Well, if you build a snow woman and try to shag it, what do you expect?' David replies.

At dinner one of our Sherpas, Pasang Lama, tells me about his ascent of K2 last year, on the night of a tragedy that killed many climbers. On August 1st, 2008, eleven climbers died after a large serac above a feature called the Bottleneck Couloir collapsed, sweeping away the fixed ropes placed for their safety. Pasang lost his ice axe, and his friend Chiring Dorje descended the couloir with Pasang attached to his harness. They were with a Korean team, three of whom died, along with one of their Sherpas.

I can see that he found the experience traumatic. He finishes by saying that K2 isn't a mountain anyone should attempt unless they're able to get themselves down without the ropes. Perhaps he's right, but having abseiled down the Banana Ridge on fixed ropes, I know it would have been risky for me to descend that section without them.

In terms of objective danger the ascent of G2 is much safer than K2. Climbing the Bottleneck Couloir, with its ever-present risk of falling ice, has been likened to a game of Russian Roulette. This suggests that K2 is a suicidal mountain to attempt – even the best climbers in the world have to take great personal risk, and are at the mercy of factors beyond their control. It's not one for me.

DAY 23
ARRIVAL OF THE JET STREAM

Friday, 3 July 2009 – Gasherbrum Base Camp, Pakistan

Day three of doing nothing. Four different weather forecasts are circulating around camp, from Bracknell, Innsbruck, Berne, and somewhere in America. They all tally with each other, but none of them match conditions on the ground.

It continues to snow all day. The forecasts say it will persist until the 6th, when conditions are due to improve. Afterwards, we will need to wait a couple of days for the snow to consolidate before we can make any further progress on G2.

More of a concern than the snow is the jet stream, which is forecast to hang around the Karakoram until the 13th. This brings ridiculously high winds that will flatten campsites, blow climbers off mountains, and create deep cold – making frostbite a virtual certainty. If this happens, we won't be making any summit attempt for at least ten days. The question is whether it's worth climbing up to the higher camps if we're only going to have to come down again. On the other hand, it's hard to see that languishing at Base Camp doing nothing for ten days is going to help much, either. It's frustrating, but this is the world of high-altitude mountaineering.

I spend most of today playing cards. Gorgan is getting very excitable and competitive over our games. Most people are frustrated there's not enough sun to generate the solar power for them to check emails. I seem to be the only person in camp who couldn't care less if I don't read a single email until the expedition finishes.

DAY 24
EVER-CHANGING PLANS

Saturday, 4 July 2009 – Gasherbrum Base Camp, Pakistan

It continues to snow, and every day brings new weather reports and adjustments to our plans. Meanwhile we pass the time at Base Camp reading and playing cards.

At lunchtime Phil suggests switching our resources from Gasherbrum II to Gasherbrum I, because it's a steeper mountain and doesn't need as long for the snow to consolidate. Later in the afternoon, after new forecasts and further meetings with other teams, he is favouring G2 again. At lunchtime we are told there is only enough rope to fix the Japanese Couloir on G1, but by midafternoon there is enough to fix the whole mountain.

I'm certainly more confident about tackling G2 first. G1 is a bonus peak for me – it may prove too difficult, and I don't wish to risk my life on steeper sections where there is no fixed rope. I imagine I'd feel under more pressure to attempt these sections if G1 becomes our main objective.

We now need several fine days to consolidate the snow on G2, and then four reasonable days to reach the summit. Another issue is the jet stream. We can't climb in it, but it will help us by blowing some of the fresh snow off the mountain and compacting the snow underneath to make it less avalanche prone. It's due to hit both mountains between the 9th and 13th. We are now looking at the 15th as a possible summit day on G2.

The weather has been hard on us, but we still have plenty of time and can afford to be patient.

At dinner Phil tells us about the avalanche on G2 in 2007.

'I brought a load up to G2 and was heading back down again when the German team decided to head up to Camp 3, after we'd told them it wasn't safe. I remember looking up and seeing their leader doing this.'

He makes a tugging gesture with his right hand. I look across at Gordon and see a glimmer light up in his eye. I'm certain he's about to make an inappropriate joke. Luckily, he doesn't, because as soon as Phil continues the story, the mood in the dining tent becomes a lot darker.

'He's tugging on the fixed rope to try and pull it out of the snow. Suddenly it's like the whole slope above Camp 2 comes loose. I'm descending the couloir at the time – we didn't use the Banana Ridge that year – and the avalanche comes over my head. I can see two German climbers fly past me waving their arms and legs. They're completely buried by the snow and we never find their bodies.'

The avalanche was huge, and the area above Camp 2 became a technical rock climb rather than a steep trudge through snow. Expedition teams switched over to Gasherbrum I if they had permits, or simply went home. This is one of the reasons Phil decided to get permits for both mountains this year.

'I hope no idiots trigger an avalanche this year,' Phil murmurs.

By the end of dinner our mood has brightened. It's US Independence Day. Phil, as a Brit who has lived in New York for over twenty years, is the nearest thing we have to an American in our team.

'Can I serenade you with bagpipes?' Gordon says.

'Bagpipes? What the hell are you talking about?' Phil replies.

Gordon holds his nose and karate chops his throat while humming *The Star-Spangled Banner*. By the time I head back to my tent for some sleep, this incident is all I can remember of the evening.

DAY 25
WATCHING THE WIND

Sunday, 5 July 2009 – Gasherbrum Base Camp, Pakistan

At night the wind hammers on my tent for some hours. It's so strong that I can hear it through my ear plugs, but I remain warm and comfortable inside my down sleeping bag.

By morning there's a fresh layer of snow on the ground, the thickest since we arrived here in Base Camp. Gorgan and Philippe intended to go up to Camp 1 this morning, but they're still here at breakfast.

By eight o'clock it's a fine morning again, and I walk up the moraine to seek the view of Gasherbrum II up the South Gasherbrum Icefall that we're lacking from Base Camp. Every time I've tried this journey so far I've been thwarted by low clouds in the Gasherbrum Cwm, so this morning I set off straight after breakfast with Ian and Michael. Ian takes the safer undulating route up and over each moraine hump, but I decide to look for a flatter, more direct route by breaking trail through thick snow to the left of the moraine. I must be careful on this route, as I need to distinguish snow from glacier and look out for crevasses.

After twenty minutes or so, Philippe catches up with me. He is armed with a trekking pole for probing in front of him, so I let him take over the lead. After a few close encounters with crevasses – one of which swallows Michael's leg – Philippe stops at a spot looking right up the icefall.

Although the sky is cloudless, the fresh snowfall is evaporating off the mountains, obscuring Gasherbrum IV. Even through slight haze, the view of G3 and G2 is fantastic. We can see the whole of the route up G2 from just below the Banana Ridge to the summit. The slopes look dangerously overloaded with snow, and a cloud plume on the top half of the summit pyramid is the telltale sign that fierce jet stream winds are battering it. Despite the fine weather down here at Base Camp, it's still not the time to be attempting G2.

Lenticular cloud batters the summit of Gasherbrum I

The weather remains stable for the rest of the day, but we need a few more of these to make the mountain safe again. We also need the jet stream to move off the summit. Our patient vigil will have to continue a little longer.

DAY 26
THE VIRTUES OF PATIENCE

Monday, 6 July 2009 – Gasherbrum Base Camp, Pakistan

It's a second day of fine weather. After breakfast, Michael, Ian and I set off down the moraine through the rest of Base Camp in the direction of Concordia. Tents are strung out a long way, and it takes us nearly half an hour to pass the last of them as we climb up and down mounds of moraine on our way out. My plan is to see if there's a way across the Abruzzi Glacier on moraine to the foot of Chogolisa, a striking triangular mountain rising above Base Camp at the point where the glacier turns a corner on its way back to Concordia.

Chogolisa has a rich history. The great Austrian mountaineer Hermann Buhl fell and lost his life there just two weeks after making the first ascent of Broad Peak. He was the only person to make a first ascent of an 8,000m peak solo, when he climbed Nanga Parbat in 1953. Initially the answer to my question appears to be positive – there does look to be a line of grey humps crossing over the glacier to the mountain's base. But after an hour of walking, Chogolisa has disappeared into cloud and we still haven't reached the corner. We turn around and head back. It's likely we'll have many more spare days to come back here if we want to.

Back at Base Camp, Gorgan is entertaining three people from other teams in the dining tent. He tries to pretend that we're leaving for the icefall tomorrow, but I don't believe him. He's by far the most restless member of our team, and he believes we should be making forays up the mountain rather than sitting around Base Camp waiting for a weather window.

The rest of us are more patient. With all the snow that has fallen in the last week, we couldn't possibly have gone above Camp 2 on Gasherbrum II. I'd far rather wait in comfort down here than in a haring blizzard high up. Although the weather forecasts change a little every day, they've generally been accurate. Two things will halt our progress no matter what: lots of snow and the jet stream. We still have time on our side. We're now waiting to see how much snow gets deposited on the 9th, when another dump is predicted.

In the afternoon Phil comes running out of his tent with perhaps the most positive news we've had for a few days. His business partner, Jamie McGuinness – whose data has so far been accurate – has emailed to say there looks to be a weather window beginning on the 12th. We're keeping fingers crossed that our patience will be rewarded. In the meantime most of us have decided to go up to Camp 1 tomorrow just to stretch our legs and keep acclimatised. This will be my first bit of serious exercise since I came down from Camp 2 on the 30th, a week ago.

Ian is concerned about his 101-year-old grandmother, who fell and broke her arm while we were in Skardu. He has sent her an email, and called her on Arian's satellite phone. Now he has decided to make her a get-well card, which he's sent back to Askole with some returning climbers in the hope they can post it in Skardu or Islamabad.

'Did you just send her a card?' Gordon asks in sinister tones while he is slowly dealing out a round of cards. 'My grandmother always prefers cash… and she gets very upset if we don't give her enough… She's a sweet lady… except when she's been drinking…'

Ian seems at a loss quite how to answer this.

'Just a card, Gordon,' he says eventually. 'I only have rupees.'

DAY 27
A LEG STRETCH TO CAMP 1

Tuesday, 7 July 2009 – Camp 1, Gasherbrum Cwm, Pakistan

We start out at five o'clock from Base Camp, just as it's getting light. Phil, Ian, Gordon, Arian, Michael and I make good time through the icefall in pleasant conditions. It looks like it's going to be another beautiful day. The sky is clear, but Gasherbrum I obscures the sun as we make our way up, so we climb in shadow. Although it's cold, movement keeps us warm, and the sun's rays touch the top of Chogolisa and Baltoro Kangri behind us.

About halfway up I rope up with Arian and Michael. Arian is leading, and he maintains a steady but comfortable pace. Sunlight radiates across the line of jagged teeth that is G5, G4, G3 and G2 directly ahead of us. We remain in shadow until we're nearly at the top of the cwm, and this time we make it to Camp 1 in just 4¼ hours.

Even better than this is the amazing discovery that for the first time in three ascents, I've reached Camp 1 and I'm not completely exhausted.

It's 9.30 when we arrive, and the sky remains clear till shortly after midday. A metre of snow surrounds our tents, and we spend some time digging them out while Phil and Gordon head over to the lower slopes of Gasherbrum II to assess the avalanche risk.

Figures on the glacier, with Gasherbrums V, IV, III and II up ahead

I'm no avalanche expert, but as I dig out our tents I can tell that the snow has not consolidated yet – it sits easily in light slabs one on top of another as I shovel away. When Phil and Gordon return from digging a pit at the bottom of the south face, they confirm that it will need at least another 24 hours of consolidation. We will have to keep our fingers crossed there's no more heavy snow, or we may have to abandon our attempt on G2 and switch to G1.

Phil, Gordon and Ian head back down to Base Camp at one o'clock, but Arian, Michael and I have decided to take it easy. We're going to spend another night up here and descend tomorrow, giving us an extra night of acclimatisation at nearly 6,000m. We all seem to be in good physical shape for a summit attempt now, and it's a shame the weather is denying us an opportunity to climb.

We only have a single stove at Camp 1, so later in the afternoon Arian squeezes into the tent with Michael and me. We risk trying a new brand of freeze-dried expedition food, and enjoy a surprisingly tasty meal of soup, chapati with cheese, and chicken and rice washed down with coffee.

DAY 28
KIDNAPPING THE COOK

Wednesday, 8 July 2009 – Gasherbrum Base Camp, Pakistan

Arian wakes me at five o'clock by shouting from the neighbouring tent.

'It was minus eighteen last night!'

I look at my watch, but it reads just -8°C, which seems more likely. It's been -7°C at a similar time in the morning at Base Camp, which is 850m lower and consequently some 5° warmer (you can usually reckon a drop of 6°C per 1,000m of altitude gained). I'm getting used to the cold temperatures now. It's next to impossible to put on boots, harness and crampons and go for an early morning slash without ending up with freezing fingers. Usually I clear this discomfort quickly after I put on my big down mitts and start walking. But it's another crystal-clear morning and I'd like to be able to take photos, so I take a chance with my small leather Marmot gloves.

Arian, cheerful as ever, jogs up and down on the spot while he waits for Michael and me to get ready. We leave Camp 1 at six o'clock. Michael leads this time, with me in the middle of the rope and Arian at the back. My fingers are painful at first, but after twenty minutes of arm-swinging I manage to get them comfortable enough for photography.

I soon discover that taking sneaky pictures while on the move isn't quite so easy from the middle of the rope. For most of the walk down, Michael's silhouette is framed above by the giant sun-kissed dome of Baltoro Kangri (or Golden Throne), which sits above Base Camp on the opposite side of the Abruzzi Glacier. This mountain frequently lets us know it's there by giving off avalanche rumbles. We can see more of it – a good 500m crowning its top – from the upper reaches of the South Gasherbrum Glacier. Peering at the camera display with a rope swinging in front of me, another swinging behind, and an ice axe under my arm is a tricky operation. I can only risk it on the more open sections where we are free from immediate crevasse danger. Even so, on a couple of occasions Michael has to stop when my legs get entangled and he feels a tug on the rope.

About half an hour after we've left camp, we encounter a cheerful Serap Jangbu coming the other way with our cook Ashad. Ashad has worked Base Camp on many expeditions, but this is the first time he's come up to the Gasherbrum Cwm. Although we're perturbed that Serap has kidnapped our cook, the smile that lights up Ashad's face as he stands beneath the horseshoe of triangular peaks quickly dispels any hard feelings.

We get back to Base Camp at 8.45. The others have waited for us before having breakfast. At 9.30 Serap and Ashad stroll back into camp, having left at three o'clock in the morning, walked all the way up to Camp 1 and come back down again. We expect such feats of stamina from Serap Jangbu, the man who's climbed eleven 8,000m peaks, but given that it took me six hours just to get up the first time I went to Camp, 1 it seems we have a superstar chef in our midst as well.

It was a great couple of days in the Cwm, and very encouraging for the summit push, but I have no difficulty falling back into the lazy routine of Base Camp life. I hang all my gear up on the outside of my tent, lie inside reading *Tom Jones*, then watch Gorgan get over-excited by a game of cards in the dining tent. There are times when it's like watching a small child throw its toys out of the pram. If we were stuck here for six months, I'm certain Gorgan would be the first to go insane, and end up putting his underpants on his head and a pencil up each nostril.

Lots of attention is focused on the fixed ropes on the Banana

Ridge, which are now buried under snow. I overhear someone come over and describe them to Phil as being 'buried beneath at least two sun crests' (he may have meant two snow crusts).

Adele from Jagged Globe has gone up today with two HAPs (High-Altitude Porters) to see if she can locate the anchor points; and Gombu and our Sherpa team will be going up with a spade tomorrow to try and re-establish the trail.

We're still looking at a July 14th summit attempt, and a complete day of sun today will have gone a long way towards making the route safe again. But six days is such a long time in the Karakoram, and anything can happen between now and then.

DAY 29
UELI STECK

Thursday, 9 July 2009 – Gasherbrum Base Camp, Pakistan

As I spend another day lazing at Base Camp, Gombu and Pasang are busy preparing the way for our summit push. They leave Base Camp early this morning, travel past Camp 1, and excavate all the buried ropes as far as Camp 2. At Camp 2 they discover our tents are submerged under two metres of snow. After digging them out and re-pitching them, they go up to Camp 3 to pull up all the fixed ropes on that part of the route as well. Despite this unimaginable feat of endurance – which would leave me dying of exhaustion before I'd left Camp 2 – it wouldn't surprise me to see them back at Base Camp in time for dinner.

Leaving aside the five Sherpas in our team (Gombu, Pasang, Tarke, Temba and Serap), two climbers stand head and shoulders above the other eighty-odd climbers here with permits for Gasherbrum I or Gasherbrum II. While some of our teams are transparently commercial groups who provide support services on the mountain for relatively inexperienced climbers to have a better chance of reaching the summit, other teams consist of so-called 'independent' unsupported climbers.

But at times it's hard to see the difference. Apart from carrying up and pitching their own tents, which our Sherpas do for us, the independent climbers don't seem to be doing much more than we are. They are all waiting for our Sherpas or Jagged

Globe's HAPs (High-Altitude Porters) to break the trail and fix ropes for them. Most have provided our two teams with hardware such as ropes and snow pickets, and others have paid to used the fixed ropes. Many of them come to our camp every day to find out the specialist weather forecast that we're paying for. One pair of Portuguese climbers even sit in our dining tent having tea and biscuits that Ashad and his team always provide for them.

Even within our team Gorgan and Philippe are supposed to be paying for 'base camp only' services, but they seem to be on much the same schedule as the rest of us. All of our schedules are dictated by our Sherpas breaking trail and fixing ropes – though to give Philippe his due, he has hired Serap Jangbu to help him, whose presence has benefited all of us.

The two notable exceptions are the Finnish climber Veikka Gustafsson, who is currently breaking his own trail up Gasherbrum I to complete his 14th and last 8,000m summit, and the Swiss climber Ueli Steck. Ueli is famous in European climbing circles for a series of record-breaking speed ascents on a handful of mountains in the Alps. He is the subject of much speculation today. He broke his own trail to Camp 2 on Gasherbrum II yesterday, and he was seen above Camp 3 today. Some say he even climbed the rock pyramid to the summit rather than traversing beneath it on the standard route that the rest of us intend to use. I expect all will be revealed in the next day or so.

To pass the time before we begin our summit push, Ian, Gordon, Gorgan, Michael, Arian and I play the longest game of cards in Gasherbrum Base Camp history. Starting straight after breakfast we play twenty-eight hands and finish just before lunch at one o'clock. In terms of stamina, Ueli Steck has nothing on us. Ian, who has a reputation for being rubbish at cards, wins convincingly.

Later in the afternoon I'm involved in an incident of supreme idiocy when I walk into the dining tent and spy a half-eaten tin of sardines on the table. The rest of the team are gathered around Phil's tent, deep in conversation. The sardines remind me of the old student prank of taking out the bottom drawer of a chest of drawers, putting an open tin of fish underneath, and replacing the drawer. The unfortunate victim then has to live with a deteriorating fishy smell for the rest of term.

I pick up the tin of sardines and carry it over to Gorgan's tent, intending to slide it under his back porch. Unfortunately I don't notice that I'm carrying it at a slight angle, and I only discover my mistake when I arrive at the tent to find a revolting odorous fish sauce covering my trouser leg. As these are supposed to be my 'clean' trousers, I immediately go to the glacial stream beneath our campsite to wash the offending stain off with soap and water. The people crowded round Phil's tent notice me doing this, and Gorgan of all people starts shouting at me.

'Mark, don't do it, don't do it!'

I return to my tent to dry off my wet trouser leg, but it still stinks of fish after it's dried. I spend the next hour contemplating the poetic justice of my backfired schoolboy prank. I can feel the karma building deep within me, and I eventually decide to sneak back to Gorgan's tent and sheepishly remove the sardines.

DAY 30
WASTE MANAGEMENT ON 8,000m PEAKS

Friday 10 July, 2009 – Gasherbrum Base Camp, Pakistan

It's a day of anticipation and waiting around. Tomorrow, at long last, we embark upon our Gasherbrum II summit push. I get a fair way towards completing *Tom Jones*, but I don't manage it, and the ending will have to wait until I return next week.

In the afternoon, a group of porters from the K2 Clean-Up team, whom Arian and I spoke to when we passed through Concordia, arrive at Base Camp to do some litter picking. The front entrance of my tent is tied open, so I see them pass by as I read. I'm not the only one, and I hear cries across the campsite.

Phil: 'Arian, are you going to give them a hand?'

Gorgan: 'Yes, Arian, you've done nothing!'

Gorgan is alluding to Arian's statement at the start of the expedition that he would be helping to clean up the mountain as a complement to his master's dissertation about waste management on 8,000m peaks in Pakistan. He has interviewed most of the teams about their waste-management policies, but in the three weeks we've been here none of us have seen him carrying out any more waste management than we have. We've all picked up the few bits of litter we see in the immediate vicinity of our tents, and carry down any rubbish we create at the higher camps.

I would not be surprised if his earlier resolution to

concentrate on cleaning up Camps 3 and 4 will be discarded in favour of a summit attempt with the rest of us. I can't really blame him for this, as I'm doing nothing more myself. But his earlier talk has left him open to criticism. Perhaps more importantly than this, he's obtained sponsorship in the form of free clothing from mountain equipment manufacturers on the strength of his clean-up operations on other mountains such as Aconcagua in Argentina. He will have to do something more, but perhaps he already has something in mind and we do him an injustice.

Later in the afternoon some Pakistani liaison officers begin clearing away an area of moraine next to Ian's tent. They are going to pitch some tents of their own, and we're told there will be a party here tomorrow night.

'It's the only time in the year the Pakistanis drink booze,' Phil says. 'I'll be there.'

Until now Ian has been dithering about whether he will leave early tomorrow for Camp 1 with Michael and me, or whether to delay his departure until midnight with Phil, Gordon and Arian, and climb directly to Camp 2.

Gasherbrum Base Camp with Chogolisa rising up behind

'You'll be able to get pissed and leave for Camp 2 straight from the party,' I tell him.

I've bet myself a fiver that Ian, who doesn't believe in making things easy for himself, will end up plumping for the straight-to-Camp-2 option, but I think this new development might sway him the other way.

Veikka Gustafsson came back down to Base Camp today. He'll be launching his summit bid on Gasherbrum I at the same time we launch ours on G2. Everybody seems to agree that the summit window has finally arrived. Yesterday Ueli Steck was the first person to summit G2 this year after breaking trail on his own from Camp 1. He passed us on skis while we were digging out our tents at Camp 1 three days ago, but he agreed with Phil and Gordon that the slopes to Camp 2 were still unsafe, and came back again half an hour later. He must have decided things were better the following day, the 8th. He climbed to Camp 2 (and possibly up to Camp 3 as well) before reaching the summit and returning to Camp 2 yesterday. It was a superhuman effort given the conditions that we witnessed from down here.

Phil went to see him after he got back to Base Camp today to find out what the snow was like above Camp 3. He said Ueli was looking extremely weather-beaten, but that's hardly surprising given that the jet stream seemed to be hitting the mountain during his climb. He must have reached the summit in very high winds. He told Phil the snow isn't too bad on the Traverse – only about 20cm deep – but it's approaching waist deep on the summit ridge.

At dinner Phil brings less encouraging news in the form of an updated weather forecast. Conditions for our summit day on the 14th seem to be deteriorating. The prediction yesterday was for winds of twenty to forty km/h, but now they've increased to thirty to fifty. Wind speeds on the 15th are now estimated at fifty to seventy km/h, and seventy-plus the day after. Phil is now considering a ten o'clock evening start on the 13th for our summit attempt. This will involve walking through the night to reach the top as early as possible on the 14th. It won't be much fun, but it means we can be on our way down again before the winds get too strong.

We're now looking at frostbite territory on summit day. Phil gives those of us attempting an 8,000m peak for the first time some tips on how to avoid it.

'If you want to go to the bathroom, don't undo your down pants and pee normally, or your dick's gone. Instead, piss inside your down suit – you can always clean it later.'

It sounds like wise advice. It also confirms that Phil is more American than British. We Brits would be surprised to see a bathroom at 8,000m.

The change in wind speeds has put a dampener on spirits and dented our confidence prior to launching our summit push. But there's nothing we can do about it. The 14th is our only possible window, so we've just got to get on with it and hope things turn out all right.

DAY 31
STARTING THE G2 SUMMIT PUSH

Saturday, 11 July 2009 – Camp 1, Gasherbrum Cwm, Pakistan

We head back up to Camp 1 for the fourth time. It's overcast and surprisingly mild when I wake at four o'clock this morning, with a balmy temperature of 2½°C inside my tent. Michael is fast asleep, and there's no response when I call him from outside. I have to go inside his tent to wake him up. Likewise Gorgan has to rouse the kitchen crew to bring us tea and hot water, though in fairness to them they respond quickly and it doesn't delay our departure.

Michael, Ian and I begin our summit push on Gasherbrum II shortly after five o'clock. There are lots of people in the icefall this time, and most of them are roped together. Initially we climb unroped, and we are able to overtake them before roping up at the end of the intricate section.

The overcast conditions make the climb a little monotonous. There are no blue skies and jagged grey peaks, just an endless sea of white. At the top of the cwm, Ian and I get slightly irritated with one another. After climbing non-stop for over two hours I'm feeling pretty tired. I halt a couple of times for Michael to take photographs, but each time Ian, at the back of the rope, hassles me to keeping moving after only about thirty seconds. The path branches and I take the one that looks like a shortcut, only to arrive at the edge of a large crevasse. The 'shortcut' then loops round to join the original path at almost the same point where we left it.

'Mark, you've taken the wrong path,' Ian says from the back of the rope. This seems obvious, and I assume he's trying to wind me up.

'Would you prefer to lead?' I ask, with what I think is a measure of irony in my voice.

Ian doesn't sense it though. He turns around and starts trying to lead us back around the circle that I've just completed.

After a couple more heated exchanges, we continue on our way and arrive at Camp 1 shortly after nine o'clock. It's the quickest we've done it yet, and we're all friends again. The sun dimly penetrates the cloud cover and heats the tent up rapidly. This is the fourth time we've been here, and every time there's been a period of two or three hours over midday when it's too hot to do anything but lie in the tent and sleep. This is no great hardship; in fact, it's blissful.

We see figures on the Banana Ridge on their way up to Camp 2, but we think most people are waiting for our Sherpas (and Jagged Globe's high-altitude porters) to go above Camp 3 to fix ropes and break trail. Given the very tight summit window, it looks like it will be busy up there on the 14th.

At three o'clock it starts snowing. 'Here we go again,' I think to myself. It only lasts an hour and sunshine follows, so there is no harm done. But during the six o'clock radio call with Phil at Base Camp, David Hamilton, who is leading the Jagged Globe team up at Camp 2, comes over the air with a discouraging remark.

'Here at Camp 2 it's been very windy all day. Looking upwards it's going to be difficult to get to Camp 3 and dangerous to go any higher,' he says.

Will the wind drive us back, and is our summit attempt doomed? Afterwards I step outside our tent and gaze around the Gasherbrum Cwm, something I never tire of doing. I can see what David means. Here at Camp 1, all is tranquil and the sky above is predominantly blue. But some of the summits, such as G4 and G1, have nasty black clouds hanging over them. Fast-moving grey clouds pass left to right above G2's shoulder, the place where Camp 3 is sited.

We get into our sleeping bags in a sombre mood. We are expecting to be woken at four o'clock tomorrow morning by our companions, who will be leaving Base Camp on their summit push at midnight.

DAY 32
SUMMIT UNCERTAINTY

Sunday, 12 July 2009 – Camp 2, Gasherbrum II, Pakistan

My alarm wakes me at five o'clock after a good night's sleep. My immediate thought is that Phil, Gordon and Arian were expected to arrive an hour ago and I didn't hear them. No more than a minute later, I hear voices outside the tent.

'Fuck me, that was tiring,' I hear Arian say.

'I'm just going to jump in here for an hour or so,' Gordon says.

Phil next: 'Guys, let's stop for a short rest, put on down suits and then move on, 'cos it's fucking freezing. It sounds like everyone is still asleep.'

Like hell we are, with the racket they're making. They left at half past midnight from Base Camp, and it sounds like they're in a bad way. I can hear Arian throwing up. Then he climbs into the tent with Phil, and I hear his voice again.

'I think I'm hypothermic.'

'Then get your down suit on, quick,' Phil replies. 'I think I've got giardia. I shat myself twice on the way up.'

I assume he means he relieved himself by the side of the trail, but I find out later it was so cold that he did it on the move – inside his clothing, like he told us to do if we needed a pee. Yeuch! Meanwhile, we don't hear another word out of the usually garrulous Gordon.

I look at my watch and see that it's reading -10°C. This is the minimum the thermometer goes down to, so it will be much colder outside. It's still dark, and the moment just before dawn is always the coldest part of the day. I'm glad we had an easy walk up yesterday, and really can't understand why Phil, Gordon and Arian decided to make it hard for themselves by leaving at midnight and climbing through the night.

I put on a few warm clothes, pull the gas canister out of my sleeping bag, lean forward and light the stove in the porch. The sound of it roaring into life attracts the attention of Phil and Arian in the adjacent tent, and I offer to make them hot drinks. Michael and I filled the tent's stuff sack with snow before we went to sleep, so we have plenty to melt for water without having to get up.

An hour later Arian has warmed his insides with hot grape juice and is ready to leave for Camp 2 with Phil.

It's still bitterly cold at six o'clock. Michael, Ian and I pack up in leisurely fashion and leave when the sun comes up at seven o'clock. Gordon is still flat out inside his tent and says he'll come later. The fixed ropes on the route up to Camp 2 mean that he can climb without a partner. Philippe and Gorgan, who also came up yesterday and said they'd leave at six o'clock, have still not arisen.

Despite the cold, it's another glorious day – clear skies and very little wind. We plod slowly up the lower slopes of Gasherbrum II, and I stop to take many photos as Ian, who doesn't really know the meaning of slow plod, starts pulling away from us. We pass a party of Iranians on the first section of fixed ropes, and are surprised to catch up with Phil and Arian, who left Camp 1 an hour before us, just below the Banana Ridge.

We complete the rest of the ascent together. The ridge is in good condition, and we plod slowly up steps on slopes of forty-five to fifty-five degrees. It's a great setting; we pause to admire the view at the top, out over the whole of the Gasherbrum Cwm and down to Base Camp on the Abruzzi Glacier. A line of climbers edge up the ridge below us.

We complete the short horizontal ridge and descend the few

metres into Camp 2, behind the rock buttress, at 10.30. Once again, it has felt like a straightforward ascent and we're full of confidence, but the weather is uncertain. Above us we can see figures on the way up to Camp 3. There are clear views up to the summit, and although the thin wispy clouds flying off the rock pyramid provide evidence of roaring winds up there, Phil thinks we can still summit in these conditions. The mood is upbeat again.

Today passes in a similar fashion to yesterday, only 500m higher up. The sun beats down on the tent in the early afternoon and we try to snatch some sleep, but with Phil, Gordon, Arian, Ian, Philippe and Gorgan all camping right next to us, there's too much conversation to sleep like we did the day before. At three o'clock the sky clouds over and it starts snowing, but like yesterday the snow lasts barely an hour before the sun comes out again.

As Michael and I sit in the tent enjoying our freeze-dried roast turkey with potatoes and stuffing, Phil does the six o'clock radio call with Jagged Globe and Gombu, who is up at Camp 3 with Pasang. We now have conflicting weather reports. One says the next couple of days are going to be bad, but there is calmer weather following. The other says the weather will be OK tomorrow, but high winds after. Neither is favourable for a summit attempt in two days' time, and more snow could increase the avalanche risk on the slopes above us once again.

Phil agrees to contact Gombu at seven o'clock tomorrow morning for an update on conditions at Camp 3. Then it will be time to make a decision.

It snows in the evening here at Camp 2, making the slopes above unstable again. At 8.30 I hear a small avalanche close by.

Tomorrow I'm expecting we will have to beat a retreat. Bummer.

DAY 33
THE BANANA SKIN RIDGE

Monday, 13 July 2009 – Gasherbrum Base Camp, Pakistan

We have a morning of waiting here at Camp 2. Several inches of snow fell overnight. It was a very mild night with little wind, but conditions are overcast above.

Gombu joins the call at seven o'clock to say it's windy at Camp 3, but he and Pasang are going to try to fix ropes to Camp 4. By 8.30 the situation has changed again. The sun comes out briefly at Camp 2, but things appear to be worsening above. At least six avalanches come down the face, and although none are on the trail itself, conditions are clearly unstable.

Then Gombu comes over the radio again to say it's now very windy up there. He says that nobody should think of ascending to Camp 3. Phil orders them back to Camp 2, but tells them to leave the fixed ropes in place. Although we must sit tight for the time being, there's still a slim hope we can go up later if the weather improves.

Things are put in perspective a little later. Phil is sheltering inside his tent when he receives a call on his satellite phone from his wife Trish to say that a Korean and a German climber have died on Nanga Parbat, a hundred miles away across the Karakoram. The Korean woman Go Mi-sun had just completed her eleventh 8,000m peak and was due to come to Gasherbrum afterwards, where the rest of her team is waiting for her. Trish believes both fatalities occurred on the way down, and we speculate whether they were due to the jet stream.

By midday the weather has become atrocious, and we decide to retreat from the mountain. We leave in a blizzard. To make things more difficult, about thirty or forty people we had no idea were here in camp decide to head down the Banana Ridge at the same time. I don't know where they all came from – Camp 2 comprises only a handful of tents – or why they are all retreating at the same moment when they've had all morning to assess the weather. I conclude that many people on the mountain are taking their cue from Phil. Throughout the morning we could hear his voice outside the tent as he talked on the radio with Gombu and David Hamilton. When he told us to pack our kit up to descend, it seems that he was instructing many more people than he thought.

View down the Banana Ridge from the top

This is the second time I've descended the Banana Ridge in horrible powdery snow conditions. The presence of so many people makes it far more traumatic than last time, when the ropes were clear and I was able to abseil most of the way down.

We trudge up to the horizontal ridge in a whiteout, and at a painfully slow pace. We discover the reason for this at the top: an elderly German climber has lost his nerve. Instead of coming back down to easier terrain to let the queue of people past, he cowers on the ridge as we try to climb around him. Ian goes first, then Arian, then me. We each have to hold onto the rucksack of the person in front as we detach ourselves from the fixed rope, step down into the snow beneath the ridge, reach around the German climber, reattach our carabiners to the rope, and step back onto the ridge. It's a nerve-racking operation, and all the while a chill wind cuts across us.

The person in front of Ian is abseiling down the fixed line, so Ian has to wait until the rope is clear. In the powdery snow conditions abseiling is much the safest way to descend, but people are queuing up behind us. Phil shouts for Ian to drop down as quickly as possible so that everybody can get out of the wind.

Again I begin the painstaking descent, facing into the slope and edging down step by step with the front points of my crampons. I feel for a stable foothold and pray that the snow doesn't give way beneath me. I yearn to abseil, but I know this means the climbers above me won't be able to share the rope, and I would keep them waiting until I reach the bottom. This is fine when the ropes are clear, but with so many people waiting in precarious footholds. it would be selfish and dangerous. Yet I know I'll find it gruelling, if not impossible, to front-point all the way down the 200m ridge.

But if I'm still thinking of abseiling, Phil makes me change my mind in his usual brusque manner. The person in front of Ian is taking an age to abseil down.

'These people shouldn't be on the mountain,' Phil cries. 'They should learn to climb before they come here. Even on Everest people are better than this.'

He's probably right, but I have doubts whether I'm a good enough climber myself to down-climb the entire ridge in these conditions.

'Do a forward rappel instead,' he says.

'What's a forward rappel?' I shout back up.

Gordon is next but one behind me, and replies on Phil's behalf.

'Put your ice axe away, face outwards, and walk down using the rope as a handrail, but don't put all your weight on it.'

This is easier said than done. My crampons ball up with fresh snow, causing my feet to lose traction. Every step is like treading on banana skins. With my ice axe tucked inside my harness, I can't bang it against my boots to dislodge the snow.

I fall three times, and each time the fixed rope saves me. The first two falls happen when I'm trying to forward rappel. I find this technique impossible, and I lose my footing. The second fall is a bit embarrassing. I swing in a wide arc across the face for several metres before I'm able to find any purchase with my crampons and inch my way back onto the ridge. After this I abandon the forward rappel, face into the slope again, and resume front-pointing, with my ice axe in hand. I find this method hard work, both mentally and physically.

I tiptoe down with no safe places to stop, and my calf muscles scream in pain. Poor Arian, descending immediately below me, has the additional hazard of expecting any moment to get a crampon in his head as I lose my grip and take another tumble.

I put my third fall down to sheer exhaustion. I'm near the bottom of the slope when I simply lack the strength to keep a toehold with my crampons. The slope is precipitous now, and I let go of my ice axe. It dangles on my harness. I grab the rope with both hands and haul myself back into a stable position.

'Right, that's it,' I say, partly to Arian but mainly to myself. 'Fuck what Phil says, from now on I'm abseiling.'

But now a Polish climber immediately behind me is getting fed up with my incompetence. He gets impatient as I wait for Arian to clear the rope below me so that I can abseil.

'Please, this is the last rope. Can we climb down?'

'OK,' I reply. 'I was going to abseil, but I'll try.'

I manage to descend the next rope without falling, but at the bottom I discover there's another one. Exhausted now, and seeing that Arian has vacated the rope below, I attach my figure-of-eight and slide down to the bottom of the ridge. Here it turns a corner on a new rope. I try to abseil down this one, but in my weary state I have difficulty swinging around the corner.

The Polish climber catches up with me and shakes his head.

'No, it's easy. Easy path!'

I look down and see that he's right. Sheepishly I let him pass, detach my figure-of-eight and follow him down the slope to a flatter area. Here I unhitch my rucksack and flop into the snow.

The remainder of the descent to Camp 1 is easier, but the danger of falling remains. We are all having problems with our crampons balling up with snow, and the benefits of wearing them are debatable in these soft, powdery conditions. Some people even take theirs off, but they have just as many difficulties. I constantly bang the snow off my boots with my ice axe, only to find football-sized chunks build up just a few paces later.

Many people slide onto their backsides. At one point I hear a cry behind me and turn around to see Tarke come flying past. He makes no attempt to arrest himself with his axe, and simply sits back and toboggans down. Within seconds he's at the bottom of the slope while the rest of us struggle on down. It's oddly reassuring to discover that a man who's climbed six 8,000m peaks finds it no easier to keep his footing than I do, though perhaps Tarke has chosen the sensible option. Meanwhile, we overtake members of the Jagged Globe team, who are still abseiling, even on this gentler slope.

I limp into Camp 1 at 2.30, where we have a short rest and leave most of our things for our next trip up. I don't relish the thought of a fifth ascent through the icefall.

At 3.15 we leave Camp 1 and continue down to Base Camp. I share a rope with Michael and Ian, and decide not to wear my crampons until the intricate section, so useless have they become in the freshly fallen snow. Michael is leading this time. He sets off at a crawl, I assume for my benefit, as I'm usually the slowest member of the team.

He speeds up, but a few minutes later I hear Ian's voice

behind me.

'Michael, can you slow down, please?'

What's going on? Ian's usually much quicker than I am. Can he be ill?

But then I remember – he's carrying a big rucksack. This is his last attempt on Gasherbrum. He is due back in the UK at the end of the month, so he needs to carry all of his equipment back to Base Camp. His expedition is over, and there will be no summit for him this year.

But first he needs to get down safely. Towards the bottom of the icefall he puts his leg through a snow hole, a common occurrence here. Michael and I wait patiently for him to extricate himself. But five minutes later, as Phil, Gordon and Arian arrive on the second rope, he is still in the same position. Snow has collapsed around his leg and frozen it in place. Phil helps to dig it out for him, and we move on.

At 6.15 we stagger into Base Camp, tired and in low spirits. The weather and my difficulties on the technical section of the climb have left me disheartened. Although we still have three weeks here, I'm starting to face the prospect that we may not get a serious attempt at either of these mountains.

Veikka Gustafsson has also retreated from Gasherbrum I, and Ueli Steck's superhuman solo ascent of Gasherbrum II on the 9th is still the only summit on any of the Gasherbrums this year. Word is arriving that teams are abandoning K2 and Broad Peak too, and although Nanga Parbat has seen ten summits, two deaths were a high price to pay.

It's looking like a bleak season in the Karakoram.

DAY 34
BROODING

Tuesday, 14 July 2009 – Gasherbrum Base Camp, Pakistan

Today is one of the worst days yet. Although there's not been much snow, conditions at Base Camp are cold, overcast and windy. It's a day to sit inside your tent and do little else. The mountains all around us are invisible through a shroud of damp white mist.

Two Polish and one German climber return from Camp 1 and walk past our dining tent as we're having breakfast. One of the Poles says there was half a metre of snow overnight up there, although the German indicates a line level with the top of his boot.

The gloom is partially alleviated in the middle of the afternoon when Gorgan rouses us all from our tents with the promise of tea and chocolate cake in the dining tent to celebrate Bastille Day. True to form, the Portuguese couple – Antonio and Sophia, who are climbing Gasherbrum VI – happen to be passing our campsite at the time, and have positioned themselves right in front of the cake. They certainly have a gift for networking, but they're personable people, and nobody seems to mind.

Tarke arrives later, when there are just two pieces of cake left.

'What is this for?' he asks.

You can't expect a climbing Sherpa to be familiar with French history, so I enlighten him.

'Gorgan has asked Ashad to cook the cake to celebrate cutting off the head of his king.'

I'm still disappointed with the difficulties I had on the Banana Ridge, and concerned that I became part of the problem. Phil is bullish in defence. He insists I would not have fallen off the mountain when I slipped, and says I would have arrested myself had the fixed ropes not been there. I'm doubtful, and I know I would have found it extremely difficult to traverse the face back onto the ridge without falling again.

'We've all fallen before,' he says. 'It builds up your confidence and is part of the learning process.'

That's nice of him, but he has much more belief in my ability with an ice axe than I do. While lots of people had problems with their crampons balling up, I'm concerned by the greater difficulties I had facing outwards and standing up. I wonder if it's anything to do with the homemade anti-balling plates I made with gaffer tape earlier in the expedition.

Phil is less sympathetic when I mention this.

'Dude, you might as well blame it on the boogie. Don't blame your equipment. You need to dig in with your heels rather than your toes.'

'And why no ice axe?' I ask.

'So you can hold on to the rope with both hands rather than just one.'

'And one other thing. Why was nobody using a safety Prusik on the fixed rope? That would've arrested my fall straight away and stopped me doing that embarrassing pendulum swing across the face.'

'One extra thing to worry about,' Phil says with a shrug.

I finish the conversation with renewed confidence. While I'm not exactly looking forward to tackling the Banana Ridge again, I'm hopeful that I won't have to descend it in a powder-snow blizzard for a third time.

DAY 35
CONTROVERSY ON NANGA PARBAT

Wednesday, 15 July 2009 – Gasherbrum Base Camp, Pakistan

More information filters through to us about the deaths on Nanga Parbat, though much of it is still hearsay. We understand that the Korean woman, Go Mi-sun, died from a fall while descending from the summit in jet stream winds. But there may be other more controversial circumstances surrounding the accident.

'There's trouble on Nanga Parbat,' Phil says, emerging from his tent. 'It looks like the Austrian team pulled the ropes on the way down.'

He means they removed them, leaving those following behind with nothing to attach to.

'That's outrageous,' I reply.

But Phil has some sympathy for the Austrians. 'It's not right, but I can understand it. The Koreans are the only team here who have contributed nothing to the fixed ropes.'

Our team, Altitude Junkies, and the Jagged Globe team, have been doing almost all the rope fixing on Gasherbrum II. Phil and David Hamilton have given other teams plenty of warning that we'll remove the ropes after we've finished with them, unless they are prepared to pay for them or contribute equipment. Everybody at Base Camp has chipped in apart from the Korean team. They have been waiting, coincidentally, for the very same

Miss Go who died on Nanga Parbat to arrive and make a decision as their expedition leader. It's possible the Austrian team gave the same warning on Nanga Parbat, but the Koreans used the fixed ropes anyway. This is speculation, and Base Camp seems to be fertile territory for rumours. If it turns out to be true, removing the ropes while there are still climbers who are relying on them for descent is wilfully putting lives at risk.

'I fell three times descending the Banana Ridge the other day,' I reply. 'If somebody had removed the fixed ropes while I was still at Camp 2, I'd be dead.'

'Dude, I've already told you, you would've arrested yourself. You might've shat yourself, but you wouldn't have died,' Phil says, deftly turning an ethical debate into something more puerile within the space of a sentence. 'There's nothing wrong with that. I've shat myself on a mountain many times before.'

The moment has gone, but we have highlighted an enduring problem with commercial peaks. Things were much simpler in the days when only experienced alpinists, ready to take their own risks, climbed difficult mountains. But when climbers of differing levels of experience are on a mountain together, and they accept different levels of risk, who is responsible when things go wrong? Teams like ours are equipped with extra safety precautions, but should we all be competent enough to descend when the safety precautions aren't there?

If the answer is yes, then I, for one, should not be climbing Gasherbrum. The K2 tragedy in August last year, when eleven climbers died on a single day, happened in part because inexperienced climbers were unable to descend safely when a serac collapsed and swept the fixed ropes away.

There's also the issue of people attempting dangerous feats which are beyond their ability. Only a handful of elite mountaineers have succeeded in climbing all fourteen 8,000m peaks, and many more have died trying. But this hasn't deterred a number of lesser climbers – who like me need fixed ropes for the harder bits – from trying to tick them off. Some of these peaks, like K2, Annapurna and Nanga Parbat, can be called 'suicide mountains'. Campsites and routes are full of objective danger, and climbing them becomes a game of Russian Roulette. I find it harder to sympathise with climbers who die in these circumstances. They know the risks, but they are seeking a greater glory. They disregard the possibility that other climbers may risk their lives trying to save them if things go wrong.

Whatever the answers to these difficult questions, our Sherpa team is pleased to discover the Korean team has quit Base Camp and left behind a fresh bag of chillies.

DAY 36
THE MAGICAL RISING TENT PLATFORM

Thursday, 16 July 2009 – Gasherbrum Base Camp, Pakistan

It's a second day of good weather down at Base Camp, and I take the opportunity to re-pitch my tent. As you might imagine when there's a river of shifting ice just a few inches below it, the tent has moved a lot since we arrived, but not in the direction I expected.

It would not have surprised me to have some subsidence in the middle, where my warm body has melted the ice underneath. But in fact the opposite has happened. The whole tent has risen up on a mushroom of ice.

Unfortunately this pedestal is smaller than the base of the tent, so I'm sleeping on top of a small mound whose summit is the middle of the floor. Towards the edges of the tent, the floor falls away, producing a deep crack all the way round the perimeter. My possessions are sucked into this ditch like tramps to a gutter.

The reason for this weird phenomenon is because the tent fabric shades the snow beneath it from the worst of the sun. The sun is therefore melting the glacier around the tent more quickly than the ice underneath.

I re-pitch my tent in a dip, knowing now what I didn't before – that the tent will eventually rise up on a new platform rather than sink further into the dip. It's much more comfortable now that I'm no longer perched on a bump. I'm not as close to the ceiling, and the interior feels like a high-roofed cathedral.

I look in amazement at the old wrinkled platform I'd been sleeping on for many days. How had I managed to get any sleep at all? When I first pitched the tent a month ago it was a flat area of gravel in a slight dip, but now it's a jagged hillside lined with cracks.

My new setting means I'm no longer looking across the icefall, where I used to see little black silhouettes on their way to Camp 1. I have now rotated my tent to face Baltoro Kangri, but it feels more peaceful in this secluded hollow.

Gasherbrum I from Mark's tent at Base Camp

When the sky is clear like it is tonight, the period at eight o'clock, immediately after dinner, is a magical time. As the sun disappears behind the mountains at Concordia, most of the valley is in shadow, but the crowning glory of Base Camp – the huge summit pyramid of Gasherbrum I, with its smooth wall of snow fringed by rock borders – remains lit up like a giant floodlit edifice. Across the Abruzzi Glacier the broad dome of Baltoro Kangri remains bathed in a purple glow, and a sliver of orange light dapples Chogolisa's darkened northern flank. This heavenly light show performs for us maybe once every three nights, and it's definitely the most memorable thing I've ever brushed my teeth to.

More bizarrely, Gorgan, Arian and Michael have decided that watching me brush my teeth is good entertainment. Every evening, as I scrub away on the raised moraine outside my tent, they line up outside the dining tent and watch. Weird.

DAY 37
BASE CAMP BOREDOM

Friday, 17 July 2009 – Gasherbrum Base Camp, Pakistan

Today is the third successive clear day at Base Camp. We're getting restless at the delays, but everyone who has tried to get above Camp 1 recently has been driven back by the wind. Although it looks calm down here, appearances are deceptive, and at least the snow will have time to consolidate.

We're now talking about heading back up the mountain on Sunday or Monday, hoping the wind will have dropped by the time we get up there.

This morning I walk for about an hour up the moraine to get that one picture of Gasherbrum II from the Abruzzi Glacier while the sky is clear. Although it takes around two hours of walking to get a single photo, it will hopefully be worth the effort – and let's face it, I've got bugger all else to do today. I'm rewarded when I finally get the view I'd been hoping for – a complete panorama of G3, G2 and G1, looking up the icefall.

In the afternoon we have another marathon game of cards. I'm concerned that I'm going to run out of books before the end of the expedition. I haven't brought enough of my own for two months' reading because I assumed I'd be able to swap with other people. But apart from a copy of Bill Bryson's *Notes from a Small Island*, nobody's brought anything to read apart from trashy thrillers. For me this is only marginally more interesting than reading a legal contract.

Things have got so bad that I'm now reading Dan Brown's *Angels and Demons*, about a ludicrous plot to blow up the Vatican – a book I would never normally read in a million years. Every page turned brings me one step closer to putting my underpants on my head. It's lucky I don't have pencils to put up each nostril.

DAY 38
DEPARTURES

Saturday, 18 July 2009 – Gasherbrum Base Camp, Pakistan

I get up at five o'clock to bid goodbye to Ian and Philippe, whose expeditions are over. They will walk out with the German Amical group today.

We have breakfast in the cold and dark, and Arian is far too cheerful for that time of the morning. By six o'clock the porters have still not turned up, so I wish our two friends a safe journey and return to bed.

Ian needs to go back early to sail in a yacht race. Gasherbrum was his second attempt to climb an 8,000m peak. On Manaslu last year it was a similar story for him. He climbed no higher than Camp 2, and had to leave because of other commitments. The weather improved after he left, and those who stayed behind reached the summit a week later. What are the chances of that happening here?

Philippe has already climbed Everest and completed the Seven Summits (the highest mountain on each continent). His aim this year was to climb Gasherbrum I, Gasherbrum II and Broad Peak. Now there's no longer time to climb all three he feels like he's failed, so he's going home without climbing any of them.

The Jagged Globe group are also leaving tomorrow, and shortly before lunch a rumour reaches us that they have books they want to leave behind. Excited, I walk over to their camp with Gorgan, only to be given five more trashy thrillers and an autobiography of Jeremy Clarkson, the whining automotive journalist. I would rather read a car maintenance manual.

I've now finished *Angels and Demons* and have moved on to reading *Patriot Games* by Tom Clancy. Lord give me strength. It's certainly better than *Angels and Demons*, but towards the end it descends into a lengthy siege involving gun-crazy American servicemen saving the Prince of Wales – *our* Prince of Wales I should say – from the IRA. One of the Americans ends up lecturing the poor prince on the best policy to appease the terrorist threat. The book was written in the 1980s, and I can't help reflecting on the irony of it all. God bless America.

DAY 39
WAITING ON THE WEATHER

Sunday, 19 July 2009 – Gasherbrum Base Camp, Pakistan

Phil is beginning to get frustrated about the accuracy of weather forecasts. Lots of people from other teams are going up and down the mountain, while we've chosen to stay at Base Camp and wait things out. Today is our sixth straight day here. Although it's been mostly fine and sunny throughout that period, nobody has reached the summit on either Gasherbrum I or Gasherbrum II.

Every day we've had reports of people driven back by the wind. Today was no different. The Iranian team was poised at Camp 3 on G2 overnight, and our very own Serap Jangbu Sherpa was at Camp 3 above the Japanese Couloir on G1, but both had to retreat. Nevertheless, the clock is ticking, and the forecasts have not been completely accurate.

Some of the forecasts are indicating that the jet stream may finally leave the Karakoram towards the end of the week. We're now thinking of leaving Base Camp for a summit push on Tuesday, with a view to staying up there and waiting for a window if necessary.

This morning, all of us – clients, Sherpas and kitchen crew – help in a team effort to move the dining tent a few metres away from a newly formed crevasse that it's in imminent danger of falling into. My one bit of exercise this afternoon involves wandering around on the glacier near my tent. I've cobbled together some new makeshift anti-balling plates for my crampons, and I want to make sure that they don't interfere with grip.

DAY 40
A THIEF ON THE MOUNTAIN

Monday, 20 July 2009 – Gasherbrum Base Camp, Pakistan

Today is our last day at Base Camp for a while. Although the weather forecasts are not promising, we are in agreement that after a week of stagnation, we need to get up the mountain and take our chances. Other groups have been doing this, and it's time for us to follow their example.

So far this year, apart from Ueli Steck's solo performance, there has not yet been a single summit on Gasherbrum I, Gasherbrum II, Broad Peak or K2. Three people have died on K2, and we think one person has died on Broad Peak. There was also a report that many people tried to summit Broad Peak a couple of days ago but had to be rescued by groups off K2. None of us has much confidence about the summit push we're about to embark on.

There have been reports of thefts from the higher camps, of food, stoves, gas, tent poles, and even some personal items like gloves. The prime suspect is a lone independent climber known as 'Polish Tom', who has been seen climbing up and down the mountain with a fun-sized pack. He carries no tent of his own, and stays in whatever tents are pitched and vacant in the higher camps. He has no qualms about making use of the equipment he finds there.

The Canada West group had a week's supply of food go

missing, and we're all expecting to find things stolen when we go up tomorrow. Although everybody thinks they know who the culprit is, there doesn't seem to be anything they can do to stop him. His trekking agency is a company called Jasmine Tours. Their 'team' has no expedition leader and consists entirely of so-called independent climbers. Other than sharing base camp services, they have no connection with each other. Thefts have even been reported within their group.

This morning, Arian, Michael and I go out onto the glacier for a refresher in crevasse rescue from Gordon, who is a volunteer with the British Columbia mountain rescue service. Crevasse rescue is a complicated procedure. It involves rigging an elaborate pulley system using Prusiks and carabiners to pull a potentially unconscious climber out of a crevasse. I've been taught the technique a couple of times before, but I'd never be able to remember all the steps in a live situation.

Gordon's session is by far the most comprehensive I've had. We're on the ice for more than two hours, and we each get an opportunity to rig the whole contraption up ourselves. Who knows, maybe this time some of it might stick.

I ask Gordon whether most of his rescues are of climbers or skiers.

'Actually, most of them are just walkers who have got lost,' he says.

The session is notable because it shows that Gordon has a serious, sensible side too. Most of the time we see an impish, bearded leprechaun sitting in the dining tent, sipping tea, and making cheap knob gags while we play cards. It's reassuring to know that his personality is much deeper than this.

Meanwhile the news from higher up the mountain is mostly doom and gloom. John, the leader of the Canada West group, reports that two Polish climbers were descending from Camp 3 on G2 when they triggered an avalanche. They would have been swept off the mountain were it not for the fixed ropes they were attached to. There have also been reports of climbers avalanched in the Japanese Couloir between Camp 2 and Camp 3 on G1, a feature we'd previously believed too steep to be a major avalanche risk.

But just before dinner we learn that a group of Iranian climbers reached the summit of G2 today, despite the winds. According to the report we've received, they set off from Camp 3 at midnight and reached the summit at one o'clock in the afternoon. This is a desperately long summit day. It is partly accounted for by the several hours it took to fix the summit ridge – none of their team had much experience of fixing ropes. We don't know how long it took them to descend again. The news that ordinary amateur climbers have finally reached the summit, despite less-than-ideal conditions, gives us hope that our summit push may not be another forlorn attempt.

But it's worth pointing out that there's nowhere like Base Camp for rumour and gossip. Every day we hear stories that are later contradicted or denied. The story about the Iranian climbers reached us by word of mouth from more than one source, and it wouldn't surprise me if it proves to be hogwash.

At dinner a friend of Phil's called Tunç Fındık (pronounced 'Tunch') joins us. He is a professional mountaineer from Turkey and has just arrived here after failed attempts on K2. He is looking to climb G2 as a consolation.

He is amiable, and keen to get to know our Sherpa crew. Prior to K2 he climbed Dhaulagiri in Nepal, another 8,000m peak. He says that a high avalanche risk made it dangerous between Base Camp and Camp 1. He has been up to Camp 2 on G2 in the last couple of days, and tells us about a new hazard on the Banana Ridge. Apparently somebody decided to relieve themselves on the fixed ropes. They left behind a brown substance so unpleasant that people prefer to detach their jumars and climb that section unprotected rather than plough straight through it.

I ask Tunç to confirm an old urban myth about the manager of the Welsh national football team.

'The manager of Wales is a man called John Toshack,' I say.

I study Tunç carefully for any sign of a reaction. He remains impassive, so I continue.

'At one stage in his career, he went to manage the Turkish side Besiktas. But he had to leave because in Turkish "toshack" means "bollocks".'

Tunç's expression doesn't change, but he gives me the answer I am looking for.

'Yes,' he says, 'this is absolutely true.'

DAY 41
THE IRANIAN GARBAGE INCIDENT

Tuesday, 21 July 2009, part 1 – Camp 1, Gasherbrum Cwm

Every crevasse, serac, undulation, stream and snow hole on the trail through the South Gasherbrum Glacier has become familiar. Occasionally the path changes to divert around a crevasse which has become too wide to leap over. Sometimes a thin layer of ice crumbles and a new stream appears. Today we have to scramble over a tumble of ice slabs that have fallen across the path. Despite these changes, however, the general route has remained the same. By this time next year every ridge and crest will have vanished and a new route will have to be found.

Today, Michael, Arian, Gorgan and I make our fifth climb through the icefall, and perhaps our last. Phil and Gordon, perversely, have decided to come up later in the afternoon. They will arrive in Camp 1 this evening.

We set off at six in the morning. We find the ice is rotten at the bottom of the icefall, but the path is still surprisingly good. It's another decent, clear day and unusually warm, but lenticulars and wispy cirrus clouds race past high overhead. Wind speeds near the summit are still a major concern.

As we approach Camp 1 in the Gasherbrum Cwm at 10.30, Gorgan and Arian start abusing a group of Iranians who are sitting outside their tents with all their food spread out on a mat of blue canvas.

Passing between seracs in the icefall

'You are disgusting!' Gorgan cries at them.

I think I hear some expletives too. This leads me to believe these people are their friends and it's just a round of friendly banter, but the Iranians remain silent. One or two of them look shocked.

'Would you like me to come to Iran and throw rubbish all over your country?' Arian says.

Michael and I look on in silence, but Gorgan and Arian are enraged. We walk over to find out what's going on. They tell us they have just seen the Iranians casually emptying a sack of rubbish down a crevasse. As Gorgan continues to hurl abuse at them I try to lead him away. It seems to me they have understood the point he is making, and there is nothing to be gained by continuing to harangue them.

Eventually the incident passes and we focus on more mundane matters. Gorgan's posh toilet, which he dug in the snow last time we were here at Camp 1, has had some use in the intervening days. Now it requires some repair work. The hole has become too wide for any but gymnasts to use with comfort. It's necessary to perch on the edge where it's slippery like a polished marble floor, preferably gripping an ice axe to steady yourself. A comical accident seems inevitable, but I get the job done without mishap. I'm relieved that I won't be needing to use it for a while (if you'll forgive the pun).

Later in the day we see twelve small figures making their way down from Camp 3 to Camp 2. One of the Iranians comes over to ask if we have oxygen. They say that one of their group is struggling, and has taken five hours to descend just a hundred metres.

It looks to us like they're descending more quickly than that. The figures we've been watching are the climbers who we believe reached the summit yesterday. They're now at Camp 2 and have found some oxygen they would like to use, but it's not ours. They ask if we can radio down to Base Camp and find out from the owner if they can take it. We think it belongs to the Canada West group, who plan to use it for their own summit attempt. We know Phil will not be pleased if we radio down for help and get his Sherpas dragged into a rescue operation. We offer them Diamox and high-altitude drugs for cerebral and pulmonary edema, but they decline.

All is quiet at Camp 1 for a while. Then at five o'clock everything kicks off.

DAY 41
DEATH OF A CLIMBER

Tuesday, 21 July 2009, part 2 – Camp 1, Gasherbrum Cwm

I'm outside the tent collecting snow and talking to Gorgan, Arian and Michael. We are looking at the mountain and watching the climbers come down from Camp 2, when the Portuguese couple, Antonio and Sophia, come over in distress.

'One of our friends is missing,' Antonio says. They start talking together and the message is garbled, but they are clearly upset.

'His name is Luis and he was climbing with Tomasz,' Antonio continues. 'Tomasz turned round at two o'clock and Luis went on, but although Tomasz looked for him for four hours, he never came back to the tent.'

'We climbed with him here last year,' Sophia says, 'and he was obsessed with reaching the summit. My god, he's gone and got himself killed.'

My first instinct is that Antonio and Sophia have heard some snippet of information and have jumped to conclusions. I've never known anywhere like Base Camp for rumour and gossip. People overhear snatches of conversation over the radio, climbers who meet each other on the mountain exchange Chinese whispers, and very little information ever seems reliable. About ninety per cent of what I hear in Base Camp about climbers' feats, incidents or weather conditions is later contradicted. Yesterday we heard that five Iranians reached the summit, but we still don't know for certain whether this is true.

We try to calm Antonio and Sophia down. It seems that two climbers, Luis and Tomasz, tried for the summit yesterday with the Iranian team, and one of them, Luis, hasn't returned. But we don't know for certain that he has died. He could have crawled into a tent and be sleeping somewhere while nobody has noticed. But Antonio and Sophia have been told there are no tents at Camp 4, not even old abandoned ones from previous years. Everyone who attempted the summit yesterday stayed at Camp 3, and the Iranians have all packed up and left – we've been watching their progress down to Camp 1 for the last few hours. That leaves Tomasz and Luis, who were sharing Luis's tent at Camp 3.

'Could Tomasz have left early this morning and Luis crawled back to the tent later?' I ask. 'Perhaps he's now safely in his tent at Camp 3.'

'It's possible,' Antonio says, 'but I don't know…'

As we speak the first Iranians are arriving back in Camp 1. Arian greets one of them as Ali.

Sophia rushes over to him. 'Have you seen the Spanish?'

'He is missing,' Ali says. 'He is gone. We got within fifty metres of the summit, but then… very technical rock climb. Everybody turned back except the Spanish. We tell him not to go, but…' He throws his arms up in the air in a gesture of despair.

Not far behind him is Luis's companion, Tomasz, who turns out to be none other than the notorious Polish Tom. He leans heavily on his trekking poles as he trudges into camp. He isn't wearing any gloves, and his hands are black and calloused. He looks tired and emotionally drained as we descend upon him to hear his story. His English isn't fluent, but we are able to understand him clearly enough.

'We reach final part of summit at two o'clock. I plead with him, I say, "please, Luis, don't go."' Polish Tom puts his palms together in a gesture of supplication. 'Then I say, "Luis, don't go up or I kill you."' He puts his fist to his chin, as though to punch himself. 'But still Luis insist, so I say, "OK, I wait for twenty minutes." But I wait three, four, five, six o'clock.' He counts the hours out on his fingers. 'I shout his name, "Luis, Luis," but still he not come. So I go.'

He is distraught, and finds his words with great difficulty. It's possible that he blames himself for not stopping his friend, and perhaps he thinks we too are blaming him for what happened. But it sounds like he did all he could. Despite the rumours we have heard about Polish Tom's respect for personal property, I feel sorry for him.

A little while later the doctor from the Iranian team arrives and confirms the story.

'We all turned around, but the Spanish went on, though we told him not to. We got back to camp and he never returned, so we were flashing our lights into the darkness to try and bring him back, but nothing. It was very windy up there, sixty to eighty kilometres an hour, and after dark it was very cold. There is no way he could have survived a night up there.'

Antonio and Sophia, and to a lesser extent Arian and Gorgan, seem to be unhappy with the Iranian team. They feel they should have done more to help, but I'm not so sure. The Iranians tried to persuade him to turn around, but if he refused, a single independent climber is not their responsibility. With poor weather conditions, high wind speeds and cold temperatures, they cannot linger without risking frostbite, and they would need to get back to camp as soon as possible. Once down, it would be several hours before the Spanish climber's absence became a serious concern, and they would be putting their own lives at risk to go back up to the summit when still exhausted from their climb. But they didn't give up: they flashed their lights to guide him down. It's hard to see what else they should have done.

'At least they could have stayed at Camp 3 an extra day to wait for him,' Gorgan says.

I'm not so sure. It's easy to judge when you're not in that situation yourself.

'You heard the opinion of the doctor,' I reply. 'He's unlikely to survive a night up there.'

'But it's funny why the five Iranians sitting here at Camp 1 never said anything to us about the missing Spaniard when we arrived,' Michael says.

'Well, that's hardly surprising – the first thing we did was give them a truckload of abuse about dumping rubbish in a crevasse. They're hardly going to strike up a conversation after that.'

Despite the desperate scenario, we keep hoping the Spanish climber is still alive. Gorgan brings out his binoculars, and Michael scans the route below the summit for any sign of a person. At the right-hand side of the summit pyramid, just below the point on the horizon where the rocky summit ridge meets the top of the snow slope, he sees a small black object which could be a person – but could also be a rock. It appears to be stationary. I peer through the binoculars myself and agree with him. A few minutes later he notices the object is no longer there, but another small object has appeared a little further along the slope. I look again and decide that if the object is a person then they are lying down in the snow, but it doesn't move for a long while, and eventually we stop watching it. Landslides and avalanches are two a penny here, and perhaps this is just a boulder that rolled a few metres down a steep slope after the snow melted. There is certainly not enough evidence to justify a rescue operation, putting other lives at risk.

Meanwhile Antonio and Sophia are still upset with the Iranian team. They say a report has reached Base Camp that someone saw the Spanish climber fall to his death after a cornice collapsed beneath him.

'Why do they make these stories up?' Antonio says, anguished.

'For them it is just, "we reached the summit, we reached the summit."' Sophia says.

This seems harsh, and I say so. 'We get these stories at Base Camp all the time. Who knows where they come from, but there's no reason to suspect it's anything sinister.'

It's common to look for someone to blame after a friend has

died. It's understandable, but it's wrong to blame the Iranians. It's obvious they are also upset about what's happened. They were subdued when they returned to Camp 1. They haven't been triumphantly celebrating their summit success – they've admitted that they didn't reach it. Ultimately, only one person is to blame for the Spanish climber's death, and that's himself. He insisted on climbing a hard technical rock section at 8,000m, without any fixed rope or protection, when everyone else urged him not to.

View of the route above Camp 2 on Gasherbrum II

To reinforce this opinion, Ali and the leader of the Iranians come over to us a little while later. The leader speaks to us in his own language, and Ali interprets into English.

'Where is Phil?'

'He will be arriving this evening.'

'Are you going on summit push now?'

We nod.

'Because we get weather forecast from University of Tehran. Very accurate, and they are telling us there is terrible weather for the next three days, but after that it is better.'

There is a well of painful emotion in the Iranian leader's eyes. 'We had terrible weather conditions and it is getting worse. We command you, please do not go up until Saturday.'

Phil arrives with Gordon at 7.30pm. He's fallen into several snow holes on his way through the icefall, and is in a very pessimistic mood. We tell him about the weather forecasts we've been hearing, and ask if we can stay an extra day in Camp 1 to delay our summit push and wait for better weather.

'Dude, I'm going to stay up here a couple of days, and then I'm going back down again. I've had enough of this weather. I don't think the jet stream's going to move off the mountain. The forecasts have been saying it will for weeks now, but the weather window keeps getting pushed back. Now it's happening again.'

It looks like Phil's given up on us ever getting to the summit, but then he adds: 'Gordon's going up, though, and if you decide to stay the Sherpas will probably come too.'

Phil and Gordon have received garbled messages about the Spanish climber Luis. Antonio, Sophia and the Iranian leader spoke to him as he arrived in Camp 1, but gave conflicting accounts. We've been talking to people returning from the summit throughout the day, and we probably know as much as anyone. We fill him in on what we've heard.

'The trouble is, everyone's very emotional,' Phil says. 'They all knew this climber and are attached to him. I'm not attached to him. He's dead. That's it.'

Phil has seen many deaths on big mountains over the years, and carried out many rescues. Some have been avoidable, while others are just an inevitable consequence of an activity involving risk. He is not being callous, just objective. The trouble is, one of the things he said isn't true, and it's an important one.

We don't know it, but the Spanish climber is still alive.

DAY 41
A LIGHT FROM ON HIGH

Tuesday, 21 July 2009, part 3 – Camp 1, Gasherbrum Cwm

At 9.45pm we're tucked up in our sleeping bags and trying to get some sleep after the excitement of the day. It's the latest night we've had on the expedition, but it's about to get longer.

All of a sudden there are lights and voices outside our tent. Somebody is trying to wake us up.

'There is a light,' an Iranian voice says.

I sit up and open the back entrance of our tent, which faces directly onto the south face of Gasherbrum II. The night is clear. I can just make out the dark triangle of the summit pyramid high above us.

A pinprick of light is flashing intermittently halfway along the snow traverse immediately below the pyramid.

It's about four hours since Michael and I saw the black dot appear to move at the top of the traverse. The position of the light would tally with a person crawling back to Camp 4 from the base of the summit ridge.

I have my torch out, and from the tent next door Gordon the mountain rescue volunteer suggests I shine single, double and triple flashes in succession, to try and open a line of communication with whoever may be up there. Unfortunately by now half the people in Camp 1 are shining their torches, and there's no way anyone would be able to figure out if I'm trying to signal some sort of code. In any case, I have no doubt whatsoever there's someone on the traverse trying to contact us. It can only be the Spanish climber, Luis.

Michael and Arian climb out of the tents and go to wake up Antonio and Sophia, his friends. They all return a few minutes later. The two Portuguese are keen to go up right away and try to reach him. Polish Tom is awake and offers to join them, and Michael and Arian are both prepared to go too. As for me, I'm sitting up inside my tent, listening to the conversation outside. I'm keenly aware that the two people in the tents either side of me, Phil and Gordon, are mountain rescue experts. I can't even begin to think how we're going to go about rescuing this person – judging by their silence, neither can they.

Eventually I hear Gordon's voice interrupt the people outside.

'Come on into the tent. Huddle round; let's think about this one.' And a moment later: 'How long do you think it's going to take you to get up to Camp 4?'

'About twelve hours,' Antonio replies. 'Eight hours to Camp 3 and another four to Camp 4.'

'And you've been up there. How far beyond Camp 4 is he now?' Gordon says.

Polish Tom answers. 'About two, two and half hours. I think he's at about 7,800m. It's very sheltered where he is, but the trouble is when he gets to Camp 4 it's very windy.'

Camp 4 is to the left of the summit pyramid, before the beginning of the traverse, where there is no rock face to protect against prevailing winds.

'So it's going to take at least fourteen hours of climbing to get to him. And when you get there,' Gordon continues, 'what are you going to do?'

'I don't know,' Sophia replies, 'but we see our friend dying up there and we have to do something.'

Nobody can argue with this sentiment, but if I went all the way up from Camp 1 to Camp 4 in a single push – 1,500m of ascent at a very high altitude – then I know what kind of state I'd be in. Even if I made it I'd need to flop straight into a tent and rest. And I'm aware that there are no tents at Camp 4.

Phil decides it's time to speak.

'It took twelve of us to carry someone down from Everest this year, and that was just 400m. This guy's nearly 2,000m above us. Michael, Arian, I don't want you going all the way to Camp 4. You've never been that high before. We don't know whether you'll be able to acclimatise, you might get cerebral edema, and then we'll have to rescue you as well. Gordon, what's the highest helicopter rescue ever attempted?'

'The usual cut-off is 20,000ft. They can fly higher than that to have a look around, but to actually pull someone off the mountain, 20,000ft is standard.'

This is about 6,000m, only a little higher than our position here at Camp 1. It means that in order to evacuate the Spanish climber by helicopter we would pretty much need to carry him all the way down here from above Camp 4. Of all the people sitting here debating, only Polish Tom has been above Camp 2 on the current expedition.

As I sit in my tent and reflect on this fact, Phil spells the situation out to everyone else.

'Right, that means we've got to get him all the way down the Banana Ridge to Camp 1. Antonio, this guy's your friend, right? Can you contact the Spanish team? They need to coordinate this – he's their climber. Ask them what they want to do. Get them to send their high-altitude porters up here immediately. Tell them to ask Hunza Guides [their Pakistani trekking agency] to contact the Pakistan Army to send a helicopter fly-by at first light [5am]. We can drop oxygen, food, water, and a radio – this will get to him far earlier than if anyone walks up there. We can also see if this guy's still alive and whether it's worth coordinating a full rescue. It's dangerous to go up there at night and puts other lives at risk.'

'OK, yes, I will,' Antonio says. 'But Phil, please can I ask, will the Sherpas be going up?'

This is the one question that hasn't been mentioned yet, but we've been thinking about it. It will take a Herculean effort for any of us to get up to the Spanish climber in a single push. In all probability, it's beyond the strength of most of us. Of all the teams on Gasherbrum this year, Phil's Altitude Junkies team is the only one with climbers realistically capable of carrying out a rescue. If anyone is going to get the Spanish climber down the mountain, then our Sherpas are going to be the ones to carry out the lion's share of the work.

We all know this, and Phil is understandably touchy about it. Because we are the only team with Sherpa support, throughout the expedition people have expected him to take the lead on everything – rope fixing, trail breaking, and now a full-scale rescue operation to bring back a climber from another team who is not his responsibility. This is why the Iranian came over to tell our team about the light on the traverse, rather than getting in contact with the Spanish team. But several teams, including the Spanish, have brought High-Altitude Porters (HAPs) – the Pakistani equivalent of Sherpas – so there is no reason Phil's Sherpas should always be first in line to do the work.

'Let's get the fly-by arranged first,' he replies. 'I don't want to send our Sherpas up there risking their lives unless we know he's alive and we've got a clear plan of how we're going to get him down.'

I believe Phil may have another motive which he's not going to broadcast to other teams. If our Sherpas are used for a full rescue operation then it's very likely our own summit chances will be over. He doesn't want to commit them before he's discussed it with me, Michael, Arian and Gordon as the paying clients (later, we discuss it and agree unanimously that our summit attempt is irrelevant if there's a realistic chance of bringing the Spanish climber back alive, but we also agree that the ultimate decision should rest with the Sherpas themselves).

Eventually common sense prevails. We're unable to contact the Spanish team, who probably have their radios turned off. At Phil's suggestion, Antonio and Sophia agree to walk back to Base Camp to wake them up and ask them to coordinate things. They also agree to wake our sirdar Gombu to get in radio contact with Phil. Phil will keep his radio on all night – like it or not he's going to be central to any rescue.

It's now eleven o'clock, and we decide to put a brew on. We

speculate on what may have happened to the Spanish climber. Phil thinks he fell, broke something and was knocked unconscious, waking up again several hours later. This would explain why he only appeared at the top of the traverse more than twenty-four hours after he went missing, and why he appears to be moving so slowly.

This is the last time we see the light flashing on the traverse. Someone here at Camp 1 has put their head lamp on auto-flash to let the Spanish climber know he's not alone. Meanwhile Polish Tom is still threatening to go back up on his own. Somewhat comically, he eyes up the crampons outside our tent.

'I have very old crampons, and if I go back up again I will need to use these,' I hear him say to Michael.

But Polish Tom is exhausted. If he goes back up at night it's likely we'll be looking for two missing climbers tomorrow. Michael talks him out of it and hides our crampons inside our tents.

Arian and Michael have been outside throughout the discussion, and are enthusiastic to help in any way they can. The older generation of Phil, Gordon and I have remained in our tents, a lot more sceptical about the practicalities of launching an immediate rescue. Gorgan, with his ear plugs in, has slept through everything. Arian has been quite emotional. At one point he was in tears watching the flashing light, knowing that someone is dying a slow death, with little anyone can do to help. By contrast Michael has been more level-headed and practical.

'At the end of the day, I'd like to help if I can,' he says to me later when he's climbed over the brewing stove in our porch and returned to the tent, 'but I don't know the guy, and he's done something very stupid.'

The water boils and we pass hot drinks to Phil, Arian and Gordon in the tents either side of us. We fall fast asleep shortly after midnight, tucked up in our warm sleeping bags, and wondering whether a solitary person over a mile above us will survive the night.

DAY 42
A LIGHT EXTINGUISHED

Wednesday, 22 July 2009 – Camp 1, Gasherbrum Cwm

I wake abruptly at six o'clock, having slept well. Snow is hammering on the tent. It would have been light an hour ago, and I didn't hear the sound of a helicopter hovering overhead. When I look out of the back of our tent, I know why. It's a complete whiteout. I can barely see Gorgan's toilet eight metres from me. I certainly can't see the base of Gasherbrum II half a mile away. There's no way a helicopter could fly close enough to a mountain to find a person in these conditions.

Phil had his radio on all night, but nobody has contacted him. He says it started snowing at 3am.

The snow continues relentlessly all day, and all the while the slope above Camp 2 becomes more dangerous. There is little hope for Luis now. When Phil finally establishes contact with the Spanish team, it seems they have little motivation to launch a rescue. They have a bag ready to drop from the helicopter when it's able to fly, but they don't intend to send any team members up until tomorrow.

Unless the Spanish climber is able to crawl to Camp 3, where there is a tent and some food, hope is fragile. He is likely to be badly frostbitten after two nights in the open above 7,000m, and may not be able to operate a stove with his fingers. Then there's the ethical issue of sending people above Camp 2 to rescue him.

The slopes are now avalanche-prone. More lives will be placed at risk trying to find someone who is probably dead by now.

If the snow continues, there is no hope.

We remain in our tents at Camp 1 all day. At five o'clock the snow finally stops and briefly a window appears through the clouds on G2. It's enough for us to see the route between Camp 3 and the traverse. Gorgan and Michael look through binoculars for any sign of the Spanish climber, but see nothing.

Arian takes advantage of the break in the weather to investigate the crevasse where he saw the Iranian climbers dumping rubbish. They have packed up and left Camp 1, taking the remainder of their rubbish with them, but they put two large bags of food outside the tents of the Spanish team. It's possible they've made an arrangement with the Spaniards to give them any unused food, but it could also be a more subtle method of leaving behind stuff they can't be bothered to carry back down.

Arian and Michael walk over to the crevasse. Dressed in bright red Mountain Hardware down suits, they look like a pair of Teletubbies, but the playful appearance belies a serious task they're about to undertake, one more suited to a Womble than a Teletubby. Arian sets up snow anchors and belays Michael into the crevasse. About seven or eight metres down, Michael finds the big white sack of litter, and hauls it out again. There are about fifteen to twenty kilos in all, which they divide up between them for carrying back to Base Camp tomorrow.

At 8pm the snow resumes. There's no possibility of going back up G2 until it has had a few days to consolidate. Retreating to Base Camp is now our only option.

At 9.30 I look out the back porch of our tent to see if there is a light on high, like there was yesterday. It's overcast, and I can no longer see G2, but for about ten minutes I signal with my head torch to try and get a response. I can only guess where Camps 3 and 4 are in the murk outside, but I see no light responding through the gloom.

I'm afraid the Spanish climber Luis is gone.

DAY 43
THE GARBAGE SEQUEL

Thursday, 23 July 2009 – Gasherbrum Base Camp, Pakistan

Whatever I said a couple of days ago – about going through the icefall so many times that every twist and turn and every peak and trough has become familiar – can be ignored.

We retreat from Camp 1 at seven o'clock in a snow storm. So much fresh snowfall has obliterated the trail that I recognise hardly any of it, at least in the upper section above Halfway Camp. Phil leads the way, tentatively at first. Visibility is so poor that sometimes we can't even see the next bamboo wand through the whiteout.

These are treacherous conditions. The whole of the icefall is an intricate maze of snow bridges and crevasses, now completely hidden by fresh snowfall. Gorgan steps into the breach. Prodding away in front of him with his trekking pole, he feels around for the firmer ground of compacted snow on the old trail. He manages to guide us through with surprising speed and accuracy. Lower down, although the snow continues to fall, visibility improves to such an extent that we can see all the way through the complex section to Base Camp an hour below us.

No matter how many times I go through the icefall, and whether I'm descending all the way from Camp 2 or just from Camp 1, I always find the last half hour into Base Camp hard work. I'm so close to home, but the route ascends and descends steeply over folds in the glacier and drags on interminably. Today the fresh snow accumulates into balls on my crampons within seconds, and just for good measure I complete the descent carrying a few extra pounds on my feet. Once again I limp in to Base Camp exhausted. It's 10.30, and it's taken us three and a half hours to descend – only half an hour less than it took us to go up.

Not content with giving the Iranian team a truckload of abuse for dumping litter in a crevasse at Camp 1, Gorgan and Arian have further plans as they pass their camp just above ours on the moraine of Base Camp. The Iranians are sitting in their dining tent enjoying morning tea when our two French eco-warriors walk to the entrance and empty the two sacks of rubbish that they fished out of the crevasse. The Iranians look on in silence as Michael captures the incident on video. This is rather more confrontational than I was expecting, and I imagine there will be repercussions.

There are, but not in the way I expect.

Later in the morning an Iranian from a different team comes to our camp and asks to speak to Arian. Arian returns from the conversation with a smile on his face.

'That man is from the Jasmine group. Antonio and Sophia have just told him about what we did. He says the other Iranian team are quite big in the Iranian Mountaineering Association. They are always talking about cleaning up in the mountains. They even run a mountain clean-up day every year. He says this will be bad publicity for them and big news in Iranian climbing circles. He has asked me for all our photographs so that he can write an article about it.'

News of Arian's deed trickles around Base Camp throughout the day. People arrive at our camp to thank him. Phil has been browsing the internet and says the news is filtering through to mountaineering websites. Veikka Gustafsson's Pakistani cook comes over to shake Arian's hand. Our cook Ashad says there have been complaints about Iranian mountaineers dumping rubbish in the Karakoram for many years, and everyone is pleased it's been highlighted.

Phil gets a new weather forecast just before lunch. Although wind speeds seem to be dropping, it looks like there's going to be more snow for another week. With time running out, and the Sherpas worried about avalanches above Camp 2 on Gasherbrum II, we agree to turn our attention to Gasherbrum I, where the route is steeper and not so prone to avalanche. G1 is a more technically challenging mountain than G2, and I'm not as confident about tackling it – but I doubt if we'll get a decent summit window on either peak, so a change of scenery is fine by me.

In any case, I don't relish the prospect of descending the Banana Ridge for a third time in horrible powdery snow conditions. Although the Japanese Couloir on G1 is supposed to be even steeper, I'm prepared to give it a go if weather permits. The Sherpas will be going up to Camp 2 on G2 tomorrow to pack up our camp and bring everything down to the Gasherbrum Cwm, which serves as Camp 1 for both G1 and G2.

At dinner we're served custard blancmange in a tin we've all been using for shaving and washing clothes. It gets halfway round the table before Michael points this fact out.

'Isn't this the same tin I've been washing my underpants in?' he says.

The blancmange remains unfinished after that.

DAY 44
SHERPA BUSINESS DEALS

Friday, 24 July 2009 – Gasherbrum Base Camp, Pakistan

'I am pissed,' Dirk the German says when he comes to our dining tent with Antonio and Sophia for their daily visit to get the weather forecast.

'Have you been to see the Czech team, then?' I ask. 'I gather they've sneaked some peach schnapps into Pakistan, hidden in tonic water bottles.'

But it turns out he's annoyed, not drunk. 'No. I've been told that Polish Tom has taken a week's supply of my food from Camp 1, and has gone up to Camp 2 on G1 to join the Bulgarian team.'

Despite his transgressions, I have to admit to a sprinkling of admiration for Polish Tom. Notwithstanding the fact that he's been stealing everyone else's food and staying in their tents, he's certainly been the most determined of any of the amateur climbers here, and he's done it in the face of atrocious weather. I don't think he's been down to Base Camp for three weeks, and has been sleeping at Camp 1 or higher (5,910m) throughout that period. He joined the Iranian team in the only concerted attempt to summit Gasherbrum II – disregarding Ueli Steck's solo ascent on July 8th, but we're talking mere mortals here. They got to within fifty metres of the summit in desperate weather conditions. Now he's switched to Gasherbrum I and is joining the Bulgarian team, the Finn Veikka Gustafsson and Veikka's Japanese cameraman, on what may well prove to be the only serious attempt to summit G1. He may be a freeloader, but the man's got stamina and determination.

Prayer flags and tents at Base Camp, looking up the icefall to Gasherbrum I

As for us, although the Sherpas intended to dismantle Camp 2 on G2 today, there was more snow overnight and they decided to wait at Base Camp. There may be a weather window on G1 this weekend, though wind speeds are still looking high on the summit. Because we were concentrating on G2, we've missed it.

We are probably going to stay in Base Camp till Monday in the hope of getting a better forecast. Fat chance. Gombu summed up our experience of the Karakoram at breakfast.

'When it's not windy it snows, and when it's not snowing – too windy.'

The forecast for the next five days is high winds and snow.

Gombu and the other Sherpas eventually leave for Camp 2 after dinner. Three Spanish climbers come to our camp to see if they're prepared to bring two tents and three sleeping bags down for them as well. Gombu keeps them waiting outside our dining tent while we have dinner.

'I hope you're going to charge them for it,' Phil says.

'Oh yes, two tent and three sleeping bag will be about… six hundred dollar,' Serap replies.

'Six hundred dollars – you're joking!'

'Is no joke, is mountain,' Temba says. Everyone roars with laughter.

In the end Gombu offers to do it for four hundred dollars, but the Spanish climbers decline. I remember a muleteer on Muztag Ata offering to carry my thirty kilos of kit down from Camp 1 for thirty dollars. I thought that was a bit steep and ended up staggering down with it myself. Any price to carry two tents and three sleeping bags between four superstar Sherpas is pretty much money for old rope, but our friends obviously don't need the money. The Spanish climbers decide to go back up and fetch it themselves.

At 8pm, as I brush my teeth outside my tent, I watch four black silhouettes make their way through the icefall at a speed that would floor me after a few hundred metres. It's Gombu, Tarke, Temba and Pasang. They expect to be in Camp 1 at ten o'clock.

DAY 45
A WEATHER CHAT

Saturday, 25 July 2009 – Gasherbrum Base Camp, Pakistan

This morning's chat about the weather forecast is a good example of the sort of nonsense we've been talking all day, every day, for weeks on end.

Phil comes to the dining tent clutching a piece of paper with wind speeds and precipitation for the next few days.

Phil: 'I've got the latest weather forecast from Meteotest. If you want a realistic chance of summiting G1 then you should go to Camp 3 tomorrow.'

Camp 3 is 2,000m above us.

Me: 'Did you say "realistic chance"? You're saying we should go all the way to Camp 3 in one go?'

Phil: 'Well, there's going to be a weather window.'

He reads out the wind speeds and precipitation for the next five days. Wind speeds are in excess of fifty km/h and there's a chance of snow on all days.

Michael: 'Which day is the window?'

Phil: 'I wouldn't go on any of them. If you want my advice, I'd go after Wednesday. Wind speeds are going to drop off.'

I scratch my head and puzzle over this for a moment. There is silence, so I break it.

Me: 'So why don't we start out on Monday and make Thursday our summit day? What are the speeds on Thursday?'

Phil: 'We don't know. The forecast only goes up to Wednesday. You can go up if you want, but I would advise waiting for the weather forecast.'

My left hand isn't doing anything, so I place its palm over my face.

Michael: 'Why don't we wait for the weather forecast on Monday? If it's good we go up on Tuesday, and if it's shit, we wait.'

Me: 'If we leave Tuesday then that's Camp 1 on the 28th, Camp 2 on the 29th, Camp 3 on the 30th, summit and back to Camp 3 on the 31st, and back to Base Camp on the 1st. Our porters are arriving on the 6th. If we leave it any later then we're into the realms of last-gasp effort. We might as well go up anyway, regardless of the weather forecast. If the weather's shit, we turn back, but we've nothing to lose. It's better than sitting on our arses in Base Camp till the porters show up on the 6th.'

Phil: 'I'm not sending my Sherpas up in a whiteout. And if there's any more snow then I wouldn't recommend going up to Camp 1 any more, either. It was dangerous the other day. I'm staying here, but you can go.'

Me: 'So if the weather forecast on Monday says it's going to snow all week, we might as well pack up and leave straight away?'

Arian: 'I'm staying.'

Phil: 'Gordon, what are your thoughts?'

Gordon: 'Well, my visa expired two weeks ago, so I'm just waiting for the Pakistani authorities to show up and throw me in prison.'

We roar with laughter, though on reflection Gordon's comment is no more ridiculous than any of ours.

I'm thoroughly confused every time we have one of these conversations. Things are clearer on the days we don't get a forecast.

Every time I mention going up regardless of the weather forecast, Phil responds as though I'm one of those crazy fools who wants to reach the summit at all costs. But I'm easily the most conservative and nervous climber of us all. I'm always the first to ask about how much of the route is going to be fixed. I've been quite explicit about turning around above Camp 3 if I'm in danger of falling on steep slopes with no fixed ropes to protect me.

Phil approached me at one point yesterday and said: 'Mark, if you decide to go up in bad weather, then I'm going to insist you take a Sherpa with you.'

Did he think I might consider tackling G1 solo while everyone else, including the Sherpas, stay in Base Camp to wait out the weather? The idea's ludicrous. I might as well climb it naked for good measure.

At 8.30, immediately after breakfast, Serap looks up the icefall and shouts down to us: 'I see Gombu.'

'What are you talking about? You can't see Camp 2 from here,' Phil says.

Gombu, Tarke, Temba and Pasang stroll into Base Camp thirty seconds later. They've been up to Camp 2 overnight, packed up our tents and food, carried them down to Camp 1, then returned here. In that time they haven't slept, and they don't even look tired.

In the evening Gorgan and Serap decide they're going to have one last-ditch attempt at G1 before they go home. Dirk the German and Tunç the Turk will go with them, but we think they've missed the weather window that Veikka and the Bulgarians are climbing in. We decide to wait until the end of next week. Although Arian is tempted to go with them, Phil talks him out of it.

'By Tuesday you've got fifty km/h winds again on the summit. That's not a weather window. If you're desperate and want to risk frostbite, then go for it. But this is your first 8,000m peak and there will be other chances.'

DAY 46
VEIKKA'S LAST SUMMIT

Sunday, 26 July 2009 – Gasherbrum Base Camp, Pakistan

The Finnish mountaineer Veikka Gustafsson is attempting to reach the summit of Gasherbrum I today. If he succeeds, it will be his fourteenth and last 8,000m peak. We spend much of the morning watching the clouds on the summit and speculating about whether he will make it. The Bulgarian team assisted him by breaking trail through waist-deep snow beneath the Japanese Couloir yesterday. They are also trying for the summit today.

Veikka was due to set off for the summit at midnight. It will probably take him at least eight hours. When I get up for breakfast at eight o'clock, a large lenticular cloud is hanging over the summit. Calmer weather follows until eleven o'clock; then the clouds return. If he's timed his ascent to arrive at the top within this three-hour period then he may well have found the only tiny summit window in a month.

I hope he makes it. He seemed a decent chap when we had tea with him earlier in the month, and he's been patient enough. Last year he turned around just fifty metres from the top. He deserves a break.

But we hear no news of Veikka all day. This is odd, and leads us to conclude that perhaps he didn't make it – most people have satellite phones, and word normally spreads quickly when summits are reached. Veikka has been contacting his wife by satellite phone, and she puts any news on his website straight away. We usually find out about things like this when Phil's wife Trish sends him a text message after browsing the internet. Today she sends nothing about Veikka, but Phil is chuffed when she tells him there's a blog on another site saying, 'The most sensible team on Gasherbrum at the moment appears to be Altitude Junkies, who are waiting at Base Camp for calmer weather.' This statement appears to be based on the evidence that Phil hasn't posted a dispatch to his website for a few days.

Arian and Michael have plans for Phil's tent

Later in the afternoon Phil goes down to Canada West's camp to get hold of their battery. They're going home today and don't need it any more. Michael and Arian are bored and looking for something new to occupy their time. While Phil is away they decide to chip away at the ice around his orange dome tent, to perch it even more precariously on its mushroom of ice. Phil doesn't notice any difference when he returns, but hopefully he'll see the funny side when he watches the video of their handiwork on YouTube.

Maturity at Base Camp seems to be inversely proportional to

boredom. For a few days now Phil has been threatening to abandon the expedition if anyone puts jelly or blancmange on his crampons again. Apparently it's difficult to scrape off in the morning after freezing overnight. I'm curious whether he's reported this in his expedition dispatches, and how it squares with the assertion that Altitude Junkies are 'the most sensible team on Gasherbrum'.

At eight o'clock in the evening Phil gets on the radio to Gorgan and Serap at Camp 2 on G1. He learns that Veikka and his Japanese cameraman are also there, having summited earlier today. The four Bulgarian climbers are up at Camp 3 – they also reached the top. It's great news. Summits at last. Are there more to come?

DAY 47
FOCUSING ON GASHERBRUM I

Monday, 27 July 2009 – Gasherbrum Base Camp, Pakistan

It looks like another clear day on the summit of Gasherbrum I, although it's windy down here at Base Camp. Phil has received a report from Veikka that there is now a technical rock section on the Japanese Couloir, and Gombu says it's going to be too cold for the Sherpas to fix ropes above Camp 3. Phil is now talking about switching back to Gasherbrum II – he thinks parts of the route on G1 may be too technical for us.

He's getting restless now the weather at Base Camp has improved slightly.

'Who's up for going to Camp 2 tomorrow?' he asks after breakfast.

'Why don't we wait for today's weather forecast, like we said we would on Friday?' Michael says.

'Dude, we're running out of time. And the weather forecasts aren't always accurate. We may as well try using chicken bones.'

'Or tea leaves,' I say, looking into the bottom of my mug.

'What do they tell you?' Gordon asks. 'You will meet a tall dark stranger who looks like Sergeant Bilko and keeps changing his mind?'

This is a little unfair – Phil does look like Sergeant Bilko, but he only keeps changing his mind because circumstances keep changing. This is part and parcel of mountaineering. But we all laugh anyway.

We have a meeting outside Phil's tent when the forecast comes through at four o'clock. Stormy weather is predicted for two days, but then the winds die down towards the end of the week. No more snow is forecast after that, and there is a glimmer of hope again – although the summit wind speeds for Friday, thirty km/h, are on the fringes of what's considered feasible.

The Sherpas don't want to go back up G2 again, so our minds are now focused on G1.

We're now one of the few remaining teams at Base Camp. The Iranian team leaves tomorrow, and tonight they have a bit of a sing-song. They take down the Iranian flag from the pole on the moraine hill dividing our camps. There are rather a lot of them, and they're making quite a bit of noise. After the garbage incident last week, we joke that they have an effigy of Arian which they're sticking pins into.

DAY 48
VEIKKA'S PARTY

Tuesday, 28 July 2009 – Gasherbrum Base Camp, Pakistan

There's doom and gloom around the breakfast table again this morning. Serap is back from another aborted attempt on Gasherbrum I, and he fell into a crevasse on his way through the icefall. He says he was in there for ten minutes, and if he hadn't been roped to the Bulgarians he'd be a dead man.

'I've never felt so scared before,' he says.

Coming from a man who's climbed eleven 8,000m peaks, including K2 and Kangchenjunga, this inevitably has an effect on the other Sherpas. They are all keen to get back to Nepal.

Gombu is on the radio to the Spanish team at Camp 1 this morning, and passes the handset back to Phil in disgust.

'Fucking Spanish,' he mutters.

Sherpas almost never swear, but Gombu has just learned that another solitary Spaniard has gone up to Camp 3 on G1 after Gorgan and Dirk decided to turn back. The rest of the Spanish team left Base Camp for Camp 1 in the early hours of the morning. During his radio call Gombu thought he could hear someone sobbing in the background. His worry is that if we all go up to Camp 2, and another lone Spaniard gets into trouble, the rest of the Spanish team will expect our Sherpas to rescue him. We're still in a state of lingering shock about what happened last week, when they made only cursory efforts to help another member of their team, struggling for his life on Gasherbrum II.

'Last week we arranged to meet Spanish team in morning to talk about a rescue,' Gombu says. 'But they not show up.'

Although weather conditions prevented a rescue and the Spanish climber was almost certainly beyond help, we expected his team to do something more. They could have sent someone up to Camp 1 to coordinate and assess the situation, and at least give a sign that they cared about him. If Gombu was annoyed with the Spanish team for not meeting him when they said they would, it's hard to imagine the feelings of the Portuguese couple Antonio and Sophia, who were friends of the climber who died. They risked their own necks by descending through the South Gasherbrum Icefall at night, then watched his team react with indifference.

Now it looks like we're watching circumstances repeat themselves.

Arian is late for breakfast. He has pains in his chest which Gordon think may be signs of a hernia. He's been on painkillers all night, and is still in pain this morning.

'Perhaps the Iranians did have a voodoo doll after all,' Phil says. He eventually gets Arian out of bed by suggesting we summon a helicopter to take him back to Skardu.

The next piece of bad news comes when Gorgan arrives in Base Camp at midday. Gordon, Michael, Arian and I are in the middle of another marathon card game. Gorgan tells us he reached about 6,800m in the Japanese Couloir. He discovered that the fixed rope is actually last year's, and is somewhat weathered after 365 days of freezing and thawing out again. Very few people have been using it this year, and Phil wonders whether it can be trusted. Gorgan also confirms that the icefall is in an atrocious state – it took him four and a half hours to descend it, instead of the usual three. Both he and Serap want to go home tomorrow. Phil's friend Tunç has already gone, after looking at K2, G2 and G1, and concluding that none of them can be climbed this year.

Later in the afternoon, Veikka Gustafsson holds a party for

everyone still remaining in Base Camp – not many of us – to celebrate his successful ascent of G1, his fourteenth and final 8,000m peak. It's a party unlike any I've been to before. There is no alcohol, men are dancing with men on a patch of bumpy moraine, and G1 forms the most amazing backdrop. The mountain looks more and more awesome every time I glance at it, probably because we're getting close to the time when we set foot on it.

The remaining cooks at Base Camp, including Ashad, have put on a good spread of food. A handful of porters and kitchen crew start banging empty fuel canisters and singing, doing their best to turn this patch of moraine, recently vacated by the Iranian team, into a dance floor. Some of our Sherpas present Veikka with a bouquet and white *kata* scarves, and he gives a short speech. He has the humility to thank the four Bulgarian climbers, who summited on the same day, for breaking trail through waist-deep snow beneath the Japanese Couloir during atrocious weather. Had it not been for them, he says, then he may not have been in place to take advantage of the narrow summit window.

And what a window. His Japanese cameraman has set up a laptop in Veikka's dining tent, and is showing footage of their time on the summit. The weather was perfect, as the jet stream winds vanished for a day. Although the summit ridge is broad enough and looks comfortable, there is one clip of Veikka hacking his way up a steep climb with his ice axe. There is no fixed rope, and it makes me nervous.

Our team is still waiting for a window on either mountain, but Veikka's film has reminded me what it can be like when everything comes together. This is why I've been sitting around on a glacier for a month and a half. Oh, to experience that crow's eye view of the Karakoram that Veikka enjoyed.

But I don't think it's going to happen now.

DAY 49
SERAP THE PHILOSOPHER

Wednesday, 29 July 2009 – Gasherbrum Base Camp, Pakistan

Gorgan and Serap Jangbu leave this morning with a handful of porters. Serap came here to climb Gasherbrum I and Broad Peak, potentially his twelfth and thirteenth 8,000m peaks, but the conditions have allowed him to go no further than Camp 3 on G1. Even so, he is philosophical, and gives a short speech at breakfast that puts things into perspective.

'There are three things which are important in mountaineering. Number one is safety. You must always come back safely and with all your fingers and toes. The mountain will always be here next year. Number two is to enjoy the climbing and your time at Base Camp. If you can't be happy in the mountains, where can you be happy? Number three is reaching the summit, and this comes only after the other two. I came here to climb G1 and Broad Peak and didn't succeed. But I am happy, because I am alive and safe, and will come back next year.'

I believe him. As he stands at the head of the table in his cowboy hat, with his long straight ponytail hanging down his back, he wears a smile that shines from his whole face, including his eyes and mouth. It's entirely genuine, and hides nothing – no regrets and no wistfulness.

Gorgan's emotions are harder to fathom.

'See you in London, when I come over to shag all your

English women,' he says with a grin as he shakes my hand. I think he's just glad to be getting out of here.

According to the most recent forecast, today is the second of three days of storms. It's certainly the worst day I can remember at Base Camp. Wet snow hammers down all day, and damp clouds hang across the Abruzzi and South Gasherbrum Glaciers, obscuring all mountains so that it looks like our little patch of moraine is afloat on an endless sea of ice. Not a hint of sun penetrates through to warm us. In the afternoon I huddle inside my tent wearing down boots, down jacket and two layers of trousers. All my tent flaps are firmly zipped up as I listen to a gusty wind hammer against the sides.

At one point a solitary wasp finds its way inside and buzzes around my ears. With not a single blade of grass for miles around, I wonder what it's doing here. Perhaps the pesky insect is as stupid as we are.

Despite the atrocious weather, our two enthusiastic youngsters, Arian and Michael, decide to spend the afternoon ice climbing on the glacier, in the expectation that it will be good practice for G1. I very much hope severe ice climbing with two technical ice axes will not be necessary. If so, I will be turning round and heading back down again. I'm older than those two for sure, but I'm still too young to die.

As I sit and listen to the snow patter on my tent, a more realistic concern is whether we will ever get above Camp 2 on either mountain. Although we were intending to put up fixed ropes between Camps 3 and 4 and on the summit ridge of Gasherbrum II, supposedly an easier mountain, I seem to be the only person concerned that none of the route will be fixed above Camp 3 on G1. Either my companions are complacent or they're talented ice climbers.

At dinner time I receive slightly better news. Phil has been over to see the newly arrived Korean team of Miss Oh Eun-Sun, who is hoping to make G1 her thirteenth 8,000m peak after coming from a successful summit of Nanga Parbat, her twelfth. Unlike anyone but us on Gasherbrum this year, she has a team of Sherpas with her – Sherpas who will be using oxygen to help them fix 400m of rope on summit day. She believes there will be a summit window between 31st July and 4th August.

Phil offers for our Sherpas to help with fixing and breaking trail, and she accepts. I try not to get too excited about this. News changes around here like a monkey swinging from tree to tree and never settling in one place. I'm certain circumstances will change again before we get anywhere near the summit. Only time will tell.

DAY 50
ICE PRACTICE

Thursday, 30 July 2009 – Gasherbrum Base Camp, Pakistan

After breakfast, while Gordon wisely retires to his tent for a snooze, I make the mistake of taking Arian and Michael up on their invitation to go ice climbing. I follow them for half an hour, all the way across the Abruzzi Glacier to the foot of Baltoro Kangri, leaping numerous icy streams en route. Here Arian stops above a twenty-metre section of vertical ice and sets up snow anchors. We abseil down to find a belay station at its base.

'I might struggle with this one,' I say to him, 'but I'll give it a go.'

I watch them climb it without much difficulty then struggle up behind them. By the time I reach the top I'm panting for breath, coughing like a smoker, and definitely not feeling like another go. Hardcore ice climbing the day before our summit push isn't what I had in mind.

'I'll leave you youngsters to it,' I say to Arian. 'I'm off back – I've got a mountain to climb tomorrow.'

He's amazed, but while he's definitely a climber, I'm just a walker who regards climbing as a necessary skill to get up certain mountains. While a climber enjoys the thrill of technical difficulty, a walker is there to enjoy the scenery and the freedom of being outdoors, and is glad to get the difficult sections over with. Happy that I've refreshed my rope skills and crampon technique, I wander back to camp.

'Those guys are a bit hardcore for me,' I say to Phil as I pass his tent. 'They had me climbing twenty-metre ice walls.'

'Dude, you don't need that,' he replies. 'That's why we take the simplest route up these mountains.'

Although we can see storms in the icefall and over Gasherbrum I today, back at Base Camp the weather holds. We're no longer receiving forecasts from our usual source, so unless the weather is atrocious when we wake up tomorrow, we're just going to head up the mountain anyway for a last-gasp effort.

After nearly two months here, I'm losing my motivation for the whole thing. I have a bad feeling about our latest summit dash, for a number of reasons:

1. Of the hundreds of climbers with permits for the five Karakoram 8,000ers this year, there have been thirteen summits and eight deaths.

2. Jet stream winds and heavy snow have been sweeping the Gasherbrums ever since we've been here. There's no indication that this is about to change.

3. One man with eleven 8,000m peaks to his name, Serap Jangbu, has already given G1 up as a bad job, and looked happy to be going home in one piece.

4. It looks like everyone left in Base Camp intends to go up the Japanese Couloir on the same day – seven Koreans, eight Spanish, seven Czechs, and nine Altitude Junkies – using last year's ropes, kicking stones and ice down as they go, and with no space for anyone to turn around if conditions aren't right.

5. There are no fixed ropes above Camp 3, and I'm conscious that at least two of the eight deaths this year have been as a result of people falling in difficult sections with no rope.

Even so, my mind is torn in two. I feel like my heart isn't in it, but neither is it in waiting down here. I have no choice, and I have to give it a try.

DAY 51
BEYOND EXHAUSTION

Friday, 31 July 2009 – Camp 2, Gasherbrum I, Pakistan

We set off through the icefall at six o'clock, for our sixth and final time. There have been reports of poor conditions from people who have been through more recently. We've never had any major difficulties with crevasses or melting snow bridges this early in the morning. We have no problem seeing them and jumping over, as long as we keep to the trail. Even so, I walk through the early part of the icefall thinking I've had enough of this mountain, and just want to get home in one piece. It's not the ideal mindset in which to start a summit push.

Towards the top, Phil suggests we rest at Camp 1 for an hour, then push on to Camp 2 before the snow which is predicted for later in the day.

I must be looking distinctly unimpressed. Knowing my preference for short days, Phil says to me: 'You're looking at me like I'm a penis.'

We arrive at Camp 1. All the Czechs and Spaniards are waiting around. They have been up here a day or two already, and the thought occurs to me that they're waiting around for our Sherpas to go ahead and break trail to Camp 2. It wouldn't be the first time this has happened. We also discover the expedition meals which the Sherpas brought down from Camp 2 are missing. While Polish Tom remains the prime suspect, several lone climbers have been making tilts above Camp 2 on Gasherbrum II through the various storms.

When Polish Tom returned from his two-week stint above Base Camp, his team's Pakistani liaison officer, inspired by Arian's example, asked him to empty his rubbish out. The liaison officer was not surprised to discover that Polish Tom hadn't brought any down with him. It helps when you can travel light by using other people's tents, gas and food, and dumping any leftovers in a crevasse.

The Koreans have been climbing through the icefall alongside us, and they stop to pitch their tents at Camp 1. But Phil wants us to push ahead this afternoon, and head up the Japanese Couloir tomorrow so that we can have it to ourselves if the other teams choose to stay here another night. There's logic in this if we're strong enough, but in my case that's not even an 'if'.

'You can go up the couloir tomorrow,' I reply, 'but I won't be going with you.'

I prefer to stay a night here at Camp 1 and go up to Camp 2 tomorrow. This is the third time Phil has suggested pushing two camps in a single day, and on both previous occasions the others ended up arriving at Camp 2 knackered, while Michael and I had no regrets about arriving the following day in good physical shape. This time Michael and Arian seem to be wavering – but Phil is insistent that everyone should push on.

'You can stay here if you like,' he says, 'but we know there's heavy snow on the way. If you want to break trail again tomorrow through all the fresh snow, that's up to you.'

In the end I realise I have to go with them. I need someone to rope up with through the crevasses, and if I don't go now then I will end up stranded at Camp 1. By the time we set off at midday, carrying the extra equipment we need for the higher camps, the snow has started falling and visibility is poor. Although he's brought four Sherpas with him, Phil ends up breaking trail himself because they're more heavily laden.

As we make our way across the thick flat snow of the Cwm to the foot of the climb up to the Gasherbrum La, Phil can barely see to the next bamboo wand in front of him. All the time I wonder why I didn't stay in camp. But whenever Phil stops and asks if anyone wants to go back, I'm the only volunteer, so we continue onward.

Then, after an hour of walking, the sun comes out suddenly and everything clears. We're still on the plateau, but now we can see the route to Camp 2 rising ahead of us. A narrow gap between Gasherbrum II and Gasherbrum I leads up through a broken glacier on a series of snow ramps between crevasses. The col ahead doesn't look that high from here, and we've been climbing imperceptibly ever since we started crossing the Cwm from Camp 1. I look at my altimeter – we're at 6,000m, and we believe Camp 2 to be at 6,250m.

We stop for ten minutes in the sun and look back across the Cwm to Camp 1. The whole area is riddled with crevasses. To our right we can now see the whole of G2's Banana Ridge in profile – from this angle it looks much steeper than the forty-five to fifty degrees I believed it to be when climbing it. Now I can see it's closer to sixty degrees. To our left, avalanches rumble down the slopes of G1 and land not far from where we sit. The setting is idyllic, but deceptively hostile.

Climbing up to Camp 2 on Gasherbrum I

The sun becomes our enemy, beating down on us as we continue up the slope, turning the hard snow into slush as Phil continues to lead. An hour or two later he stops again on a platform broad enough to seat all nine of us comfortably. We've climbed about a hundred metres and he thinks we're about halfway, an estimate that turns out to be wildly optimistic. I'm already tired and looking forward to getting the rest of the climb out of the way.

'Maria from the Spanish team says we've got to do an ice climb before we reach Camp 2,' Arian says.

I don't believe him, and think he's trying to wind me up.

'Oh, fuck off,' I gasp.

'No, she must mean after Camp 2 on the couloir, not before it,' Phil says.

Everyone nods in agreement and we move on.

Soon we have to put on crampons to climb a steep section of ice. Above it there is a crevasse across the trail. We have to leap upwards over it, a tiring manoeuvre when you're carrying a big pack under a scorching sun. Then a long, angled traverse climbs at forty-five degrees through soft snow. All the while I'm becoming more exhausted, but Temba is leading our rope, and he doesn't slacken the pace. I feel tugs in front of me as he tries to propel us forwards, and sometimes a simultaneous tug from behind as Gordon stops for a breather. It's hard work. I hear Gordon put his pack down while we're still on the steep traverse. We've been hoping for a long time to reach the brow and see Camp 2 ahead of us.

We're certainly high enough by my altimeter, but there's still no sign of the camp, and the climb has been relentless. We've slowed to a crawl, and every time I put my pack down I have pins and needles right down my forearms to my fingertips.

Gordon looks like he's going nowhere for a while. Temba suggests that he, Pasang and Arian, who are in better shape, go on ahead to pitch the tents and boil water for a brew, while Gombu, Gordon and I continue more slowly behind. I keep believing that it can't be much further to camp. Gombu's slower pace is much more comfortable than Temba's – he takes a few short steps then stops for a breath before moving again, and he keeps an eye on both of us to make sure he stops when we do.

I tell myself there's about another hour to go before we reach camp, but when we crest the rise that has been above us for over an hour, we see another long slope with an ice wall looming above. The others are trying to fix a rope up it, and we realise that at the pace we are going, there are still many hours of ascent ahead of us.

Exhausted and disheartened, we stop to consider our options. We get on the radio to Phil.

'Gordon and I are knackered,' I tell him. 'We're thinking of camping here and coming up tomorrow. Then we'll decide whether we're still going for the summit or going back down. Unless somebody can come back here and fetch our packs for us… The main thing is, whatever we do, we don't want to jeopardise Gombu's summit chances.'

'Dude, we're going to have a complete rest day tomorrow,' Phil replies. 'We're all nearly as fucked as you are. It would be best if we can all be together at Camp 2, but if you are going to camp, I'd prefer it if you didn't camp where you are. I think you might get some debris if any of the seracs on this ice wall collapse.'

As I look up at the face the others are struggling to climb, my morale ebbs ever lower, but it's a long way back to Camp 1 and I'm running out of water. Gombu gets out his stove and melts some snow to replenish our water bottles while we rest. He also gives me a Snickers bar which has melted to liquid in the hot sun, but I've not eaten since breakfast and desperately need the energy. I gratefully suck chocolate and nuts off the wrapper. When we've finished filling our bottles, the others are still struggling to fix the rope on the ice wall.

'I can tell you now, I'm not going to get up that thing,' I tell Gordon and Gombu, 'not in my current state, carrying a big pack.'

'If you dump your pack, no one's going to come back for it tonight,' Gordon says. 'They're all knackered too. We could cache most of our kit and just take the stuff we need for sleeping.'

'Mark,' Gombu says, 'if you want to camp here, then we camp here. I have tent. It's safe.'

In the end we decide to walk a little higher up the slope to the serac wall. Gordon says he thinks it will make a safer camp, but when we get there it clearly won't. With seracs behind and cracks in the snow in front indicating hidden crevasses, we'd be treading on a minefield outside our tent. We decide to push on.

The sun goes in just as we're arriving at the ice wall, and it suddenly becomes much colder. I use a somewhat unorthodox technique to climb the wall. I'm so tired that I can't contemplate doing anything too technical. I haul myself up the vertical section with my arms, using my jumar in my right hand and pulling on the rope with my left. I feel like a drunk Tarzan. At the top I collapse and wait for the others, Gombu first and then Gordon. From there it's a ten-minute walk across a wide plateau into camp. I arrive with cold fingers at 8pm after a fourteen-hour day.

It's without doubt the most exhausted I've ever been on a mountain. I've had some tough summit days, but nothing to compare with this, and we still have two hard days of climbing to go if we're to reach the summit. I look at my altimeter and read 6,450m – 200m higher than expected. It means we've climbed 1,400 vertical metres today, mostly laden down in the heat of the afternoon sun.

The others arrived an hour before us. 'Well done. Really well done,' Arian says as I approach the camp.

But I'm not in triumphant mood. 'Not well done at all. It's stupid to get so exhausted two days before summit day.'

For a day or two now I've been toying with the idea of not making another summit attempt. As I arrive at Camp 2 I feel the decision has been made for me. There are two golden rules of performing at high altitude: don't overexert, and keep hydrated. I've broken both of these today, quite unavoidably and in spectacular fashion.

I unpack all my things and, armed with a mug of hot tang Michael brewed up while he was waiting for us to arrive, I collapse straight into my sleeping bag, utterly demoralised.

DAY 52
THE JAPANESE COULOIR

Saturday, 1 August 2009 – Camp 2, Gasherbrum I, Pakistan

As if to prove a point, while I lie in my tent this morning recovering from yesterday's exertions, I hear the Korean, Spanish and Czech teams arrive from Camp 1. A combination of the trail we broke for them, walking in shade on still-frozen snow, a night of rest, and only 500 metres of ascent this morning has made the climb from Camp 1 a doddle for them.

And of course, they made use of the rope on the ice wall that I watched my team mates spend ages trying to fix last night. After attempts by several of them, Arian eventually managed to free climb the wall and fix an anchor. Bugger me, but all that ice climbing practice was actually useful after all.

It's only just nine o'clock by the time the other teams get to Camp 2. It's taken barely three hours, compared to the eight it took me and Gordon. They've arrived fresh while we have to spend a day recovering.

But it turns out the Koreans are not so wise. After a brief rest, six of the team – Miss Oh, her two Sherpas, two High-Altitude Porters (HAPs) and her cameraman – push on up the Japanese Couloir to Camp 3. I can't help thinking they're about to make the same mistake we did, and will be too tired for anything strenuous tomorrow. In fact, the task they have set themselves is even greater.

I find it difficult to leave my sleeping bag this morning. I know if I'm to push on up the couloir tomorrow I can't stay here all day. I need to get up and move. After I've lazed around for an hour or so, talking to the others through the tent walls as they watch the Koreans, Michael brings me out of my lethargy.

'Mark, you've got to come outside. The scenery's amazing.'

I know he's right. I put on my boots and down clothing, and crawl out. Camp 2 sits in the middle of a wide, flat, snowy col, and is one of those breathtaking places you know you're privileged to experience.

To the west the plateau drops away to the Gasherbrum Cwm through the ice ramps we ascended yesterday. Beyond, the broad fluted peaks of Gasherbrum VI and Gasherbrum V form a backdrop. To the east the plateau rises slightly before dropping away into China. There is nothing but a bank of puffy clouds billowing up from below. To our north are the flanks of Gasherbrum II, a forbidding wall of avalanche-ridden snow, while to the south is the upper section of Gasherbrum I, a black trapezium of rock scarred with snow chutes and icefields. A narrow cleft cuts diagonally through its centre: the Japanese Couloir, the steepest and most difficult section of the ascent.

All our attention is focused on this feature as we watch six dark figures climb it. It occupies the whole of tomorrow's ascent from Camp 2 to Camp 3, and is so narrow that it has the reputation of being a very committing climb: once you've started up with others following behind you, there's no turning back if things get too difficult.

With the Koreans out of the way, there are still three teams poised here at Camp 2 to continue their summit push tomorrow. I have an uneasy feeling about this. Miss Oh's compatriot and competitor in their race to bag all the 8,000m summits, Miss Go, lies dead after a fall on Nanga Parbat three weeks ago, and the Spanish team already has one dead member after a reckless solo attempt on G2 a week later. These are more than just omens. If twenty-odd climbers push for the summit at the same time in the high winds we're expecting, then an accident seems inevitable.

This feeling doesn't diminish as we watch the Korean

climbers ascend. In fact, it gets stronger.

The route they're taking is not what we've been expecting. Instead of going straight up the couloir, they climb a dark rock band at its base until they reach a steep snow ramp running above the couloir up to a snowfield that marks Camp 3. For some reason they are climbing this snow ramp instead of the couloir.

It takes them several hours to ascend. One figure at the back, who we later discover is the cameraman, is very much slower than the others, and drops further and further behind them. The third figure, which we assume to be Miss Oh, is keeping so close to the second one that Phil thinks she is being short-roped by one of the Sherpas (literally, pulled along on a short rope). Eventually they disappear behind a rock buttress which forms the near side of the couloir, and we can no longer watch their progress until they emerge from the other side two hours later. They are approaching the snowfield now, and nearly at Camp 3, but only five figures have appeared. Where is the cameraman?

Suddenly Gombu cries out 'Avalanche!', and we look up. Masses of snow are cascading down the ramp, directly along the route the Koreans took up it. At the bottom of the ramp a substantial quantity shears off straight into the couloir. Clipped to a fixed rope, somebody in the firing line may have been able to survive – but the avalanche looked big enough to rip out the anchors. If I had any lingering doubts about whether to go up tomorrow, this dispels them in the strongest way possible. Whether you go up the snow ramp or the couloir, it seems no part of the route is safe.

A few minutes later, a black speck emerges from behind the bottom of the rock buttress. The cameraman is descending, and it's possible his retreat triggered the avalanche. If this is the case then what might twenty people tramping up the couloir do tomorrow?

He struggles down the snow ramp agonisingly slowly; then, at the foot of the rock band beneath the ramp, he stops. Two more figures appear from behind the rock buttress on their way down. These are the two HAPs, and it becomes apparent the cameraman is stuck and is waiting for them to come and help him. Time ticks by and a cold wind blows spindrift across the mountainside. It's an hour and a half before they reach him, and by that time he must be freezing. But his ordeal is over, and we watch the three of them complete the descent and stagger into camp.

Gordon and I decide to retreat tomorrow. Predicted high winds, crowds in the couloir, a dodgy route up last year's ropes, and an avalanche straight down the route of ascent make this decision a no-brainer for us. Phil, Tarke and Gombu are of a similar mind, and decide to descend with us. Of our two young guns, Michael is wavering, but Arian is keen to push on, heedless of the many warning signs. I overhear a conversation between Arian and Gordon in the tent adjacent to ours as news comes over the radio that one of the Bulgarians has just summited G2.

'So we could have summited G2 – there was a weather window,' Arian says.

'And the Korean lady will probably summit G1 tomorrow,' Gordon replies, in apparent regret.

I'm longing to shout at them to put things in perspective. Just because someone summits a mountain doesn't mean you should have gone with them. We all have different levels of ability and willingness to take risks. The Korean lady may be prepared to die in her struggle to climb mountains, and one day she probably will. The Bulgarian has already been up G1 in the last few days, and is almost certainly a very strong climber. Like Ueli Steck, he may have climbed the ridge between Camp 2 and Camp 3 on G2 in order to avoid the higher risk of avalanches on the snow slopes of the normal route. He would have needed to free climb the technical rock section beneath the summit without ropes, a section which ultimately killed a lesser climber, the Spaniard Luis. Arian is a better climber than me, and stronger, but he's no Ueli or Veikka. This is his first 8,000m peak. I'm not convinced he realises what he's letting himself in for.

But I say nothing. He and Michael are young, strong and enthusiastic. I don't want my own caution to stop them trying what their hearts are set on. Only when Arian hears the weather forecast from the Spanish team – forty to fifty km/h winds for the next few days – and he sticks his head into our tent to ask Michael whether they should still go up, do I make a halfhearted attempt to dissuade them.

'I don't want to sound miserable, but I think you'd be stupid to attempt it. Forty to fifty km/h winds is not a summit window, and an avalanche on the route? You'll have other chances to climb an 8,000m peak.'

Yet the Spanish team still plan to ascend, and this appears to provide them with confidence, and a stronger belief that the mountain is safe. I don't think my opinion carries much weight.

Later in the evening I have another toilet ordeal. It's the first time I've worn my down salopettes when I've needed to relieve myself, and I'm not quite sure of the appropriate technique. Michael has a similar predicament, but his Mountain Hardwear down suit has zips down the side of each leg, and he doesn't have any problem when the time comes. Although my Rab salopettes have a 'shithole' between the legs, this doesn't help when you're wearing trousers underneath. In the end I have to undo the braces, loosen my jacket and then take the whole thing down in order to be sure of safety while squatting. While I struggle, one of the HAPs from the Korean team is watching from his tent. He is laughing at me, and this doesn't make the job any easier.

DAY 53
THE FINAL RETREAT

Sunday, 2 August 2009 – Gasherbrum Base Camp, Pakistan

It doesn't surprise me when I wake this morning to the sound of Michael preparing to leave. It's freezing cold, but the sky is clear and the weather seems perfect, with no sign of the forecast strong wind. Michael looks a little uncertain about whether they are making a wise decision, but Arian is keen and encourages him. Nobody else is listening to the forecast. The Spanish and Czechs are preparing to ascend, and the Koreans are already at Camp 3.

At 8.30 Arian and Michael head towards the Japanese Couloir with Temba and Pasang. Their two Sherpas are younger than Gombu and Tarke, who are retreating with us. I don't know how they feel about the ascent. For them this is a job: if two clients want to make a summit attempt then somebody has to go with them. But Temba has kids, and Pasang was on K2 last year on the night that eleven people died. He lived through it as part of a Korean expedition. A penny for his thoughts.

All is quiet at Camp 2 when Gordon, Phil, Gombu, Tarke and I leave at nine o'clock in burning sun. Before we depart, Gombu comes over and lifts up my rucksack, which is bulging with equipment.

'Too heavy,' he says. 'Nearly as heavy as mine.'

Sherpas have superhuman strength and are used to carrying

big loads. Most started their working lives as Himalayan porters, developing the right muscles from an early age. As well as their personal equipment they carry all our tents, pots, stoves and snow shovels. If my pack is nearly as heavy as Gombu's then I'm definitely carrying too much gear.

Figures make their way along the trail to the Japanese Couloir on Gasherbrum I

Today is going to be a long old slog, but we make good time down to Camp 1. At the bottom of the ice wall we see that a large section next to the fixed rope has collapsed, spilling gigantic blocks of ice over the area beneath. If anyone had been passing at the time, they would have been crushed to death. Although Gordon, Gombu and I rejected the idea of camping beneath the serac wall when we were exhausted on the ascent two days ago, it's a chilling warning of a mistake we could have made.

By eleven o'clock we've reached the bottom of the descent from the Gasherbrum La, and are crossing the Gasherbrum Cwm to Camp 1. I'm starting to feel the load on my shoulders, but there are still many hours to go if we are to return to Base Camp today.

Phil looks up and sees two figures high on Gasherbrum II, halfway along the traverse beneath the summit pyramid. We know that two Iranians and a Spaniard were at Camp 3 on G2 overnight and intended to make a summit attempt today.

'They're too late,' Phil remarks. 'They're still hours away from the summit.'

We watch their progress throughout the day as we descend to Base Camp. Four hours later, at three o'clock, we look back from the icefall just before G2 disappears from view, and see them reaching the end of the traverse. By then clouds are hammering the summit pyramid. At their rate of progress, they still have another three or four hours of ascent up the summit ridge in the teeth of a storm. If they continue then it will be well past nightfall before they're safe again. We hope they make the sensible decision to turn around.

Meanwhile we reach Camp 1 in burning sun and take a rest, collecting as much equipment as we can to take down with us. Gombu and Tarke pack away some of the tents, leaving two for Michael, Arian, Temba and Pasang. Unlike our tents at Base Camp, which rise up on icy pedestals as time passes, these ones have sunk ever further into the glacier. Great pits four or five feet deep are left behind. Since we have only used them for six or seven nights, I assume this is due to fresh snow accumulating around them.

There are two large bags of food in my and Michael's tent. I want to take as much of it as I can down to Base Camp, as I know he will be tired when he descends after his summit attempt. But my pack is overloaded, with equipment dangling from its straps, and I have to leave quite a lot of it behind.

Circumstances like these have been tempting people to dump uneaten food in crevasses, while others have adopted what they believe to be the more environmentally friendly action of donating it to teams still here. But this is a cop out – some teams have been leaving up to twenty kilos of food behind for others to dispose of. This is a full one-person load, and somebody has to carry it down eventually. We have Sherpas on our team, and while I may be taking the lazy option myself, Gombu and Tarke will return up the icefall one last time if we still have equipment to be carried down.

I know that it's going to be an ordeal getting through the icefall again, tired as I am with my heavy pack. The afternoon sun will be opening up crevasses, melting snow bridges and turning the crisp snow into slush. It usually takes us three hours to descend from Camp 1. That's not going to be the case this time.

'See you in six hours,' I shout to Gombu and Tarke as they set off ahead of us. Everybody laughs, but I'm not joking.

Still, unlike our ascent two days ago, when Gordon and I ran out of energy, I'm prepared for the ordeal ahead of us. I also know that every step is a step closer to the end of it all, that at the bottom of the icefall is Base Camp, and that after six return trips through it in the last two months, I'll probably never set foot in it again.

The Gasherbrum Cwm is one of the most beautiful, magical places I've ever seen, and at midday I leave it for the very last time.

We make slow progress, and every half hour we stop to take off our packs and sit down in the snow. I'm surprised to see that Phil, at the front of our rope, doesn't seem to be falling into as many crevasses as I'm expecting. Eventually I realise he's falling into plenty, but managing to hold his tongue. He's not spitting out the torrent of expletives that usually explode from his mouth. Towards the bottom of the icefall some of the crevasses gape open. Gordon has to take a big running leap and hurl himself across. Each time he looks back to make sure I get over safely, but I'm much taller than he is, and he's disappointed when he watches me casually step across.

Inch by inch, minute by minute, we eat up the distance, and for the last two hours we're spurred on by the tents of Base Camp on the moraine below us. At 5.30 I stagger over to my tent and ease the pack off my shoulders. The ordeal is over, and it feels great.

'I tell you, I don't envy Arian and Michael up at Camp 3 right now,' Gordon says.

Gombu and Tarke are beaming. We have no regrets about our decision to retreat.

At seven o'clock the cook from the Jasmine Tours group comes to our dining tent and tells Phil the Spaniard and the Iranians are safely back at Camp 3 on G2 having summited earlier this afternoon. They evidently don't know we've been watching them for most of the day.

'Bullshit,' I say when Phil tells me. 'There are so many liars on this mountain.'

Had they known what we'd seen, that they must have transformed from slowcoaches to supermen in the teeth of the jet stream, then they would know how ridiculous their claim must sound to us. And when they get home, who's going to care about their claim to climb a mountain nobody else has heard of? What's the point of lying about it, when the only person who cares is yourself?

Just before dinner Phil has a radio call with Arian. They are safely up the Japanese Couloir at Camp 3 on G1 and haven't been avalanched. They intend to leave for the summit at 1am, but the Korean Miss Oh has asked if Pasang or Temba can help her Sherpas to fix ropes. Phil refuses – he wants Arian and Michael to have a Sherpa each to help them. The Korean Sherpas will be using oxygen to reduce the chances of frostbite in the high winds, while our team won't.

We go to sleep worrying about what may happen tomorrow. Phil has never had a death on any of his expeditions, and I suffer heartbreaking thoughts of returning to England with Michael's kit and explaining to his family what has happened. I keep my fingers crossed his level-headedness helps to counterbalance Arian's more impetuous nature.

DAY 54
SUMMIT CONFUSION

Monday, 3 August 2009 – Gasherbrum Base Camp, Pakistan

Relief comes almost immediately this morning. Phil has a radio call with Arian at seven o'clock and discovers they are already back at Camp 3. They set off for the summit at 1.30am and walked for two and a half hours, reaching 7,300m before turning back due to the cold, the wind, and some breathing difficulties Arian was experiencing.

We understand that some of the Czech and Spanish climbers also turned around. Although it's a disappointment for them, it's good that they're safe.

We have a lazy day at Base Camp today. Phil's tent platform has now grown so large that his tent looks like a mushroom, and he needs to stand on a chair in order to climb into it. Gordon and I help him move it, and give him a hand with coiling ropes in preparation for our departure from Base Camp.

We learn that the Bulgarian did not summit Gasherbrum II. He admitted that he got to within fifty metres before turning back. There are some honest people here after all. Apparently the two Iranian climbers are still claiming they did. Now there are rumours Ueli Steck's solo ascent on July 9th is being questioned on some websites because he is yet to produce a summit photo, though Phil is convinced he made it.

We're now looking at the possibility that no one summited

173

G2 this year. Later in the afternoon we hear that Miss Oh and her two Sherpas reached the summit of Gasherbrum I with oxygen at 1.15pm, but I don't know what to believe any more.

By the evening, Michael, Arian, Temba and Pasang are back at Camp 1, where they will stay tonight. We organise our porters for the trek out – they need to set off from Askole several days in advance. Most people want to take the easy way back on the same route we came in, but Michael and I confer over the radio and agree that we would like to trek back over the Gondokoro La to Hushe. Snow is forecast for Saturday, when we're scheduled to go over. It may end up being another ordeal, but we're determined to give it a go if we can.

DAY 55
MORE SUMMIT CONFUSION

Tuesday, 4 August 2009 – Gasherbrum Base Camp, Pakistan

Michael and Arian walk into camp with Temba and Pasang at eleven o'clock this morning. They look in remarkably good shape after only taking four hours from Camp 1 in the cool of the morning, comparing favourably with our ordeal two days ago.

'It was howling at Camp 3,' Michael says, 'but we found shelter as soon as we dropped back into the couloir. Then we had to descend the fixed ropes, each time praying when we got to a new one that it wouldn't be too tight to abseil down. We were only able to abseil two thirds of it. The rest we had to down-climb. I was glad when we got to the bottom.'

'Luckily it was only me, Michael, Pasang and Temba descending at the time, so we didn't get rockfall from other climbers,' Arian says.

'Although Arian was going first,' Michael adds, 'so I kept kicking bits of ice onto him.'

'A similar thing happened to him on the Banana Ridge. There was some idiot behind him who kept falling on top of him,' I say sheepishly.

'The fixed ropes weren't too bad, though,' Arian says, smiling. 'There were only a couple of sections that looked old. Otherwise it looked like the ropes had been fixed this year, not last year like Gorgan said.'

'In fact, you usually had about five fixed ropes to choose from,' Michael says. 'None of them have been taken down from previous years.'

They don't seem too disappointed, even later in the day when further tall summit stories filter in. We hear the two Iranians are no longer claiming to have summited Gasherbrum II two days ago when we watched them on the traverse, but a Spanish climber is. He must have been wearing a white down suit on the traverse, but changed into a rock-coloured one when he reached the summit ridge. When he climbed into the storm which we saw spewing off the summit pyramid, we wouldn't have been able to see him through the clouds. This would explain why we only saw two figures on the traverse that day. His camouflage suit will no doubt be available in outdoor shops worldwide from the autumn, for those climbers who would like to climb 8,000m peaks but don't want the whole world to know about it.

Then we hear that, yesterday, the 72-year-old leader of the Spanish team went on to summit Gasherbrum I several hours after Arian, Michael, and several younger members of the team turned around. Presumably he flew there.

In fairness, many of these tall summit stories don't originate from the claimant. Some are just unconfirmed assumptions propagated as truth by Base Camp rumour-mongers. More than once, summit claims have been quashed by the very people they've been attributed to. It remains to be seen whether the story sticks of the 72-year-old Spaniard who made an oxygenless ascent of G1 in forty to fifty km/h winds on the day that strong, determined twenty-somethings turned around.[1]

---

1. This was Carlos Soria, one of the world's more extraordinary high-altitude mountaineers. He was actually 70 (and not 72) when I crossed paths with him on Gasherbrum I. At the time of writing he has reached the summit of twelve of the fourteen 8,000m peaks, and holds the age record for an astonishing seven of them. As of April 2017, he has climbed the following 8,000ers (with his age at the time in brackets): Nanga Parbat (a mere stripling of 51), Gasherbrum II (55), Cho Oyu (60), Everest (62), K2 (65), Broad Peak (68), Makalu (69), Gasherbrum I (70), Manaslu (71), Lhotse (72), Kangchenjunga (75) and Annapurna (77).

DAY 56
ACCEPTANCE

Wednesday, 5 August 2009 – Gasherbrum Base Camp, Pakistan

The rumour about the Spanish team is confirmed when they post to their website that five members of their team reached the summit of Gasherbrum I on Monday, at the same time as the Koreans. This means it took them eleven to twelve hours from Camp 3 – roughly the same time it took Veikka Gustafsson. That a 72-year-old man can climb as quickly in forty to fifty km/h winds as one of the world's best high-altitude mountaineers in near-perfect weather seems implausible, but I'm no longer sure what to believe. Perhaps he did.

Michael now tells me that he and Arian saw someone high on the summit ridge of Gasherbrum II while they were in the Japanese Couloir on G1. This supports the claim of the other Spaniard that he summited G2 while we were descending from Camp 2 on G1. It also explains why we didn't see him.

Arian and Michael started climbing the couloir at 8.30, so to be high enough to see the summit pyramid of G2 it was probably about eleven or twelve o'clock. If the Spaniard didn't get back to the traverse until after 3pm, when we last saw the Iranians at the end of it, then we wouldn't have been able to see him. Of course, there remains the question of whether he reached the true summit, or turned back at the technical section which stopped everyone else. A summit photo is the only sure proof.

177

Arian goes to the Korean camp to ask about their oxygen cylinders, which they used during their summit ascent, but we didn't see them carrying when they returned to Base Camp. One of their Sherpas sheepishly admits they dumped the cylinders below the summit, but also confirms the Spanish climbers summited when they did.

'I guess we're a bit jealous,' I say to Phil, 'but do you think these claims are plausible?'

'To be honest,' he replies, 'I don't care, as long as we're happy with our own performance and we made the right decisions. We're all back safely. That's what matters.'

'I imagine this happens on every 8,000m peak you climb?'

'Not really. On Everest and Cho Oyu there are so many witnesses around that everyone knows who summited and who didn't.'

The Spanish team return from the summit and pass through our campsite while we're sitting in the dining tent playing cards. They are tired, but otherwise they look in good shape. There are no obvious frostbite victims. They say the three Czech climbers reached the summit at the same time. This makes eleven summiteers in total – by far the most successful day in the Karakoram this year. There are too many of them for a conspiracy, and I begin to believe they did summit after all. In this case it's some achievement.

The Korean team leaves by military helicopter a short while later. For them it's been a remarkably businesslike performance. They've been here barely a week, climbed their mountain and flown out again. We're still here after two months, having climbed nothing. Even our card game is frustrating – I lose comprehensively.

'It's like a commando operation,' Gordon says of Miss Oh's ascent.

There is one further twist. Michael and Arian are sitting outside the dining tent later in the afternoon when the two Iranian climbers return from their summit push on G2. They have garlands around their necks and look happy.

'Did you reach the summit?' Arian asks them.

'Yes, we set off at 2am on Sunday, and reached the summit at 2pm.'

Phil, Gordon and I are not present to tell them that at 2pm on Sunday we saw them heading up the traverse, many hours below the summit.

I will be glad to leave this place. The scenery is breathtaking, but the people here are doing my brain in.

DAY 57
BOOK BONFIRE

Thursday, 6 August 2009 – Gasherbrum Base Camp, Pakistan

It's our last day at Gasherbrum Base Camp, and also the last day in a long while that I'll be playing cards. If I had an unlimited supply of books then I would not be spending so much time at the card table. Unfortunately, apart from the books I brought with me, the quality of literature has been absolutely terrible. As the last team to leave camp, we've accumulated a library of books so shit that nobody wants to take any of it back with them. Almost all of them are trashy thrillers with names like *Firebreak* and *Shattered Bone*.

'Buck Smith, pilot with the US Air Force, unexpectedly stumbles upon a plot to blow up New York. Injured in Vietnam and pursued by the CIA, with his knowledge of fighter planes he finds himself the only person able to save the world.'

After lunch we light a ritual pyre to burn all this crap so that we don't have to carry it back with us, though in my view some of it isn't even fit for burning, and should have been used earlier in the expedition when we were running out of toilet paper. I now have just 800 pages of book left to nurse through the remaining week and a bit before I leave Pakistan.

I spend most of the morning packing, dividing everything into a 25-kilo bag to go with the others on the normal route back to Askole, and a smaller bag with climbing kit to go with me over the Gondokoro La.

But when the porters start arriving at four o'clock, with deteriorating weather and snow forecast for the weekend, Michael decides he no longer wants to risk going over the high pass. If heavy snow were to cause another porter strike like we had on the journey in, it could mean missing our flight from Skardu, and potentially our flight back to the UK.

So we're off back on the easy route to Askole with everyone else. Secretly I'm quite relieved that Michael ended up losing his nerve before I did, but I don't tell him.

DAY 58
FROM SNOW TO RAIN

Friday, 7 August 2009 – Gore II, Concordia Trek, Pakistan

After getting up at first light, clearing away our tents and helping the kitchen crew to pack, we finally say goodbye to Gasherbrum Base Camp at seven o'clock this morning. We watch the ritual of our army of porters dividing the loads and arguing about weights. It's a much smaller army than the hundred-strong troop we came in with – this time we only need about forty.

I get bored of watching and start walking down the moraine strip that will eventually lead to home. It's a cloudy morning that threatens rain, but it holds off – at first. The grey overcast skies part briefly, just long enough for me to look back and have one final view of Gasherbrum I towering above the place that was our home for nearly two months. But before I reach the corner where the Abruzzi Glacier becomes the Upper Baltoro and turns north, everything closes up again.

It doesn't take me long to drop behind the others; just a couple of stops for photos and to remove a layer, and soon I'm on my own, following some semblance of a path on rough moraine in thick mist. A couple of times I check the compass on my wristwatch, but I can't really go wrong here. I catch up with them about an hour short of Concordia. The sun is trying to break through, but K2 and Broad Peak are nowhere to be seen among the clouds.

Concordia, the junction of three glaciers – the Baltoro, the Upper Baltoro, and the Godwin-Austen – is renowned as one of the most beautiful places on Earth, but this depends on the conditions. As we know better than anyone, the weather in the Karakoram is erratic and unpredictable. When we passed through Concordia in June, it was perfect, and the place lived up to its reputation; today it's bleak and depressing. The clouds hang low, and black rock walls are the only reminder of the mountains all around us. For the first time in two months I feel rain on my face instead of snow. A wasteland of wet black slate has replaced the white winter wonderland we walked through on our outbound journey.

The toughness of the terrain doesn't improve my mood as I weave up and down over folds in the glacier. The wind blows rain in my face as I stumble onwards. The forlorn-looking tents of disappointed trekkers spread out across the cold dark moraine; I was going to stop and eat my packed lunch here, but the rain drives me on until I see Tarke standing outside a small mess tent.

He's been looking out for me and ushers me inside. It's some kind of storage tent, and the rest of the team are crowded within, sitting on boxes and drums while Ehshan our kitchen assistant works at a stove. A mug of hot tea is thrust into my hand, and we're able to eat our lunch in the dry while we wait for the rain to slacken off.

It takes another three hours to reach Gore II camp from Concordia. Fed up with being the team slowcoach, I put on a burst of speed and manage to keep up with most of the others, but at a pace I find uncomfortably fast. In many places the slate covering beneath my feet is wearing away, exposing the smooth ice of the glacier. This means the trail is often slippery. On a couple of occasions I have to traverse the side of a steep bank of ice. Mostly I'm able to keep up with the quick pace, but the terrain is awkward underfoot.

I reach Gore II camp at 3.15, an inconspicuous area of moraine in the middle of the Baltoro Glacier. This is where we had a porter strike on the way up and had to spend an extra night. Today it's much quieter, but there are a few tents belonging to trekking groups. It's sunny when we arrive, but our quick pace means we have to wait three hours for the majority of our porters. By then a storm is brewing, and we end up putting the dining tent up in howling wind and rain. It slackens off for dinner, but heavy rain raps against our tent for much of the night.

DAY 59
BOULDER HOPPING

Saturday, 8 August 2009 – Paiyu, Concordia Trek, Pakistan

I think today is one of the least pleasant days I've ever spent trekking. The combination of lousy weather and assault-course terrain gives the Karakoram a unique place among the world's classic trekking destinations. Today exemplifies both, but I know I should look beyond this and realise that I'm lucky to be here.

I spend most of the day boulder hopping for hour on tedious hour, and by the end of it my ankles are like jelly. The main reason for the lack of a good path is because we're walking on a glacier that changes shape from season to season, but the terrain today is ten times worse than it was yesterday.

We set off in light rain and overcast conditions which persist on and off for most of the day. Gordon has twisted his knee but refuses to take a horse because he thinks Phil would take the piss out of him. At least this means there's somebody else as slow as I am. My dodgy ankles don't cope well with hours of boulder hopping.

The pair of us hobble into Paiyu camp at 6.15 after more than eleven hours of walking. I'm not looking forward to tomorrow, which is supposed to be even longer. Still, at least we're off the glacier and back on dry land for the first time in two months. Perhaps the terrain will improve.

Later in the evening Phil has a minor panic when the

expedition looks like it's about to unravel. At eight o'clock, as darkness is falling, Ashad informs him that some of the porters haven't arrived yet. If they don't show up this evening then it may mean they've done a runner with the kit they were carrying. Unfortunately one of the missing barrels contains perhaps the most important cargo of all. The entire expedition finances, amounting to several thousand dollars, are buried at the bottom of it.

There's still hope the barrel will show up after nightfall, but if the porter carrying it is still on the glacier then they've got some difficult terrain to navigate in the dark, with a high risk of broken ankles. Two of the quickest porters go back to look for them with head torches, but Phil is a worried man during dinner.

'I kept telling them to put the important gear with the quickest porters, but do they listen?' he says.

After dinner he's wandering around listlessly outside the dining tent when we hear a loud splosh, followed by expletives. He's fallen into a stream behind the campsite and cracked his knee on a rock. To cap his worry about the cash, he now thinks he may have broken something ahead of a twelve-hour day tomorrow. Ashad helps him hobble to his tent, promising to wake him with any news.

Luckily the errant porter arrives half an hour later, and all is well.

DAY 60
WATER, WATER, EVERYWHERE

Sunday, 9 August 2009 – Askole, Karakoram, Pakistan

A day of slow torture begins at 6.30am, as we conclude the trek back to the roadhead at Askole. This is not the way to enjoy trekking. The soles of my feet hurt after yesterday's extended boulder hopping, and I know this twelve-hour day is going to be sheer hell.

The first hour out of Paiyu is comfortable enough as a rocky mountainside towers to my right and provides some shade. The path drops to follow the edge of the Braldu River at the bottom of a wide river bed, before climbing high up a cliff face on a broad path; then it drops down to cross a sandy plain on a bend in the river. At the end of this the sun rises above the hillside and I stop to put on sun cream.

Here the ordeal begins.

Today's a rare day on our Concordia trek when the weather isn't cloudy. In fact, the sky is completely clear and the heat is about to become intense – and it's still only 7.30 in the morning. For the next four hours I struggle on as the trail alternately rises to become a high cliff path, then drops to meander alongside the river or cross a sandy beach. It's a big improvement on yesterday's boulder hopping, but the balls of my feet are so bruised that every step is painful. My feet expand in the heat and become uncomfortably tight inside my walking boots.

The scenery is less impressive today, but still has rugged beauty on a grand scale. The sides of the valley consist of harsh red rock, incredibly dry, while the floor is wide and flat. Although the Braldu River rarely fills its width, it contains immense rapids that could toss a truck around like a cork.

The heat soon becomes intense. To keep my momentum going and to nurse the two litres of water I have to last the whole day, I only stop for two minutes every hour, when I put down my pack and take a couple of swigs.

At midday I reach Jhola camp, our first main comfort stop and the halfway point on today's walk. It's marked by a hillside of grey Portaloos. This is where we camped on our first night out of Askole. Pasang, who is also suffering with uncomfortable footwear, lies on a roll mat in the shade of a hut. I stop for some lunch, but my chocolate has melted and the bread is so dry I can hardly eat it with my parched mouth. Gordon arrives five minutes after me. We are the three stragglers of the group. We leave Jhola together at 12.30, but we soon get separated.

Just six hours to go. I look at my watch and tell myself I can have another swig of water at two o'clock. I walk along a cliff path climbing high above the river – it's dramatic, but my feet ache in the afternoon sun and I'm unable to enjoy the scenery. By two o'clock my mouth and lips are so dry I can barely swallow. My few mouthfuls of water are like nectar and afterwards I lean into my trekking pole, inching further along the trail.

An hour later I reach an oasis in the desert that I remember from the trek in. Pasang is lying on his roll mat in the shade of a thorn tree. A stream trickles past his feet, watered by a rock cascade. I stop for a rest and some water, and Gordon joins us.

It's peaceful, relaxing, and above all, pleasantly cool. It would be easy to rest here for a long time, but after fifteen minutes I lift my pack back on my shoulders and press on along a sandy boulder-strewn trail beside the river, then across a plain that takes me an hour to cross. Halfway across, at 4.15, I stop for more water. Then I round a corner thinking it will be the last one before Askole.

The path climbs on rough steps hewn into a cliff, then back

down again to a beach. The sand is thick, and hard work to wade through. At 5.15 I stop and finish my water with the green terraces of Askole visible on a hillside in the distance. It takes me another hour to get there, on a path which climbs relentlessly. I pass some porters lapping up water from a waterfall coming down from the cliff to our right. I envy them – they have immunity, but if I were to drink the water I would probably be sick for days.

Finally the path reaches Askole and climbs through the village. Small children try to talk to me, but I'm only focused on my destination – all I want to do is reach the end of the trail. I plod past with my head down, ignoring them.

I walk into our campsite in a walled compound at 6.15. There's a subdued cheer, and Tarke thrusts a bottle of Coke into my hand. It's heaven – I don't think my throat has ever felt so dry before. I take my pack off, remove my boots, and flop down in the grass. The ordeal is over.

After two months at 5,000m, where dinner times meant down jackets, thick socks and two pairs of fleece trousers, here in Askole, beneath the trees at 3,000m, it feels positively balmy. We eat al fresco this evening after erecting our dining table beneath the trees in the warm air. As darkness falls we're still in shirtsleeves. Everyone is relieved and pleasantly tired as we eat the final meal cooked by Ashad, Ehshan and Shezad, who have been our cooks since June.

It's a magical evening. The flitter of moths around our head torches and the propane lamp in the middle of the table is a reminder that we're back at habitable altitudes again. For once the insects don't irritate me. I'm looking forward to going home, but this has been an evening to enjoy, when everything feels good with the world. The only thing missing is beer.

As we lie in the tent this evening, Michael tells me about his own experiences on the trail today. He and Tarke rounded a corner to see Gombu on all fours sucking water from a puddle no bigger than the palm of his hand. Tarke gave his water bottle to Phil, who had forgotten to pack one, and ended up licking a rock in an effort to get moisture onto his tongue. It was a day for resting in the intense heat, but somehow we've managed to walk forty kilometres.

DAY 61
THE LAST ROBBERY

Monday, 10 August 2009 – Skardu, Karakoram, Pakistan

Today is a day of mixed impressions of Pakistan and the people I have met on my journey here.

At seven o'clock we leave Askole by jeep for the hair-raising ride back to Skardu. It's less stressful this time because we meet hardly any traffic coming the other way on the single-lane track clinging high to the hillside. As the valley widens closer to Skardu we pass through villages. Our driver keeps stopping to get us handfuls of apricots from people gathering them by the side of the road. This is Ismaeli country, and although I offer money, it is always declined.

We reach hot and dusty Skardu at one o'clock. I'm looking forward to a shower and shave for the first time in two months, and to get into some clean clothes. I'm taken down to a storage vault in the basement of the Masherbrum Hotel to identify my bag, but it's not there. Not to worry, though. I recall the man in reception writing 'ATP' in chalk on my bag and putting it under the counter when I handed it over in June. It's probably been given to our expedition agent, Adventure Tours Pakistan, to put into storage.

After lunch, Phil, Michael and I wander down the high street to find the barber's shop where Arian got a haircut and shave for just fifty rupees. Their pricing is somewhat erratic, however. I relieve myself of my beard, have a no.1 cut all over, and an unsolicited head massage. I am charged 300 rupees for it. Michael is then charged 500 rupees for pretty much the same service. We attribute this to the fact that he has more hair than I do, and chooses to keep most of it.

Phil also has a shave, haircut and head massage, but then the barber gets over-enthusiastic, and starts bending Phil's arms behind his back and punching him in the back of the shoulders. Phil endures this treatment with patience, but Michael and I laugh hysterically, which only encourages the grinning barber to make the massage more extreme. I suspect it's done for my and Michael's benefit more than Phil's. When the time comes for him to pay, Phil is charged 600 rupees.

'Six hundred – but you only charged him five,' Phil says, pointing at Michael.

'But you have full massage, sir.'

Phil shakes his head with a smile. 'I didn't ask for the beating.'

He pays 500, and the staff seem happy enough.

The rest of my day is less enjoyable. I spend several hours trying to track down my missing bag, as the realisation sinks in that the hotel staff have either lost it or, more likely, stolen it. Ashad takes me to ATP's main storehouse across town to meet their storekeeper, but we can't find it there. I spend an hour in their main office eating apricots with a lady called Gerlinde Kaltenbrunner, who is aiming to become the first woman to climb all the 8,000m peaks. She has already climbed twelve. Porters stole some of her tents while attempting K2 last year, and they later turned up in a shop in Skardu. She is chasing up on the issue. Alongside her need, I suspect my little rucksack is a much lower priority. Eventually Ashad stands up and tells me we're leaving. We take a taxi back to the Masherbrum Hotel, and I don't really understand why I was taken to the office.

They all seem to be blaming each other for my bag getting lost, and nobody is too concerned about finding it. ATP's staff are more helpful than the hotel's. I wouldn't really mind, but besides my clean clothes and mobile phone, it also contains my house keys. The first thing I will have to do when I arrive home after more than two months away is call out an emergency locksmith to break into my flat and change the locks.

But when our liaison officer Major Iqbal – who has come up from Islamabad to meet us – hears about it that evening, things start to happen again. He tells me our friend Ian also lost the bag he put in storage at the hotel when he returned a few weeks ago. Suddenly everyone jumps into action, and again we head off to the various storerooms – this time with the major accompanying us. It's a nice gesture that restores my faith in people, but the reality is that the contents of my bag were probably sold weeks ago. Aside from the major, any one of the people running around looking for it could be the perpetrator. Major Iqbal is the only person I find completely trustworthy, which is probably unfair on most of those helping us. I remember seeing him at Concordia during our trek in to Base Camp, sitting outside the tents of the K2 Clean-Up Expedition and lamenting that the army is one of the biggest polluters in the Karakoram. He is one of those people who genuinely cares about things.

Ashad may have drawn a blank in his expedition to find my bag, but he's been more successful in tracking down some of the local 'Hunza Water' for the rest of the team. He and the Sherpas are sitting in Gordon and Arian's room letting their hair down for the first time in a while.

Despite not having drunk any booze for over two months, I'm not in the mood to join them. I know I will remember these days with fondness, but my overriding feeling right now is that I've had enough of Pakistan and look forward to going home.

It's a shame. The country has many things to be proud of, if only people tried a little harder. There is friendliness here in abundance, but impressions are coloured by experience, and mine today has been weighted down by people who don't care. The absence of any sort of restaurant or bar culture in places like Skardu, and the fact that women are hardly ever seen, makes the country seem excessively serious – as though there is a ban on having fun. This seems strange, because the people here – such as Ashad, with his perpetually cheerful disposition – certainly don't lack a sense of humour.

But in between the frustration and the boredom, I've rested for long periods surrounded by some of the most beautiful scenery on Earth, and for that I feel very lucky. I wouldn't swap it for anything.

It's been a long two months, and I'm glad to be going home.

ACKNOWLEDGEMENTS

Thanks to the other members of my Gasherbrum team – Arian, Gordon, Gorgan, Ian, Michael and Philippe – for being great company for more than two months, and not cheating too much at cards.

Thanks to our Sherpa dream team – Pasang Gombu, Pasang Lama, Tarke, Temba and Serap Jangbu – for their great patience when, it seemed, everyone in Base Camp was demanding their help.

Thanks to Phil Crampton for making it all happen.

Thanks to the major for being a gentleman and leaving me with good memories of Pakistan.

Thanks to my editor, Alex Roddie, for his help polishing the text.

Most of all thanks to all of you, readers of my blog and diaries. I hope you have enjoyed this one, and I look forward to welcoming you back sometime. If you have not read it already then I hope you will enjoy my first full-length book, *Seven Steps from Snowdon to Everest*, about my ten-year journey from hill walker to Everest climber.

SEVEN STEPS FROM SNOWDON TO EVEREST

A hill walker's journey to the top of the world

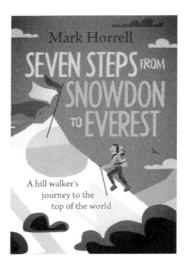

As he teetered on a narrow rock ledge a yak's bellow short of the stratosphere, with a rubber mask strapped to his face, a pair of mittens the size of a sealion's flippers, and a drop of two kilometres below him, it's fair to say Mark Horrell wasn't entirely happy with the situation he found himself in.

He was an ordinary hiker who had only read books about mountaineering, and little did he know when he signed up for an organised trek in Nepal with a group of elderly ladies that ten years later he would be attempting to climb the world's highest mountain.

But as he travelled across the Himalayas, Andes, Alps and East Africa, following in the footsteps of the pioneers, he dreamed up a seven-point plan to gain the skills and experience which could turn a wild idea into reality.

Funny, incisive and heartfelt, his journey provides a refreshingly honest portrait of the joys and torments of a modern-day Everest climber.

First published in 2015. A list of bookstores can be found on Mark's website:

www.markhorrell.com/SnowdonToEverest

PHOTOGRAPHS

I hope you enjoyed the photos in this book. Thanks to the miracles of the internet you can view all the photos from my Gasherbrum expedition online via the photo-sharing website *Flickr*.

Gasherbrum. Pakistan, June to August, 2009:
www.markhorrell.com/Gasherbrum

ABOUT THE AUTHOR

Since 2010 Mark Horrell has written what has been described as one of the most credible Everest opinion blogs out there. He writes about trekking and mountaineering from the often silent perspective of the commercial client.

For over a decade he has been exploring the world's greater mountain ranges and keeping a diary of his travels. As a writer he strives to do for mountain history what Bill Bryson did for long-distance hiking.

Several of his expedition diaries are available as quick reads from the major online bookstores. His first full-length book, *Seven Steps from Snowdon to Everest*, about his ten-year journey from hill walker to Everest climber, was published in November 2015.

His favourite mountaineering book is *The Ascent of Rum Doodle* by W.E. Bowman.

ABOUT THIS SERIES

The *Footsteps on the Mountain Travel Diaries* are Mark's expedition journals. Quick reads, they are lightly edited versions of what he scribbles in his tent each evening after a day in the mountains.

For other titles in this series see Mark's website:
www.markhorrell.com/diaries

CONNECT

You can join Mark's **mailing list** to keep updated:
www.markhorrell.com/mailinglist

Website and blog: www.markhorrell.com
Twitter: @markhorrell
Facebook: www.facebook.com/footstepsonthemountain
Flickr: www.flickr.com/markhorrell
YouTube: www.youtube.com/markhorrell

DID YOU ENJOY THIS BOOK?

Thank you for buying and reading this book. Word-of-mouth is crucial for any author to be successful. If you enjoyed it then please consider leaving a review. Even if it's only a couple of sentences, it would be a great help and will be appreciated enormously.

Links to this book on the main online book stores can be found on Mark's website:

www.markhorrell.com/ThievesLiarsAndMountaineers

Printed in Great Britain
by Amazon